First World War
and Army of Occupation
War Diary
France, Belgium and Germany

50 DIVISION
Headquarters, Branches and Services
Royal Army Ordnance Corps
Deputy Assistant Director Ordnance Services
19 April 1915 - 30 May 1919

WO95/2816/3

The Naval & Military Press Ltd
www.nmarchive.com
Published in association with The National Archives

Published by

The Naval & Military Press Ltd

Unit 10 Ridgewood Industrial Park,

Uckfield, East Sussex,

TN22 5QE England

Tel: +44 (0) 1825 749494

www.naval-military-press.com

www.nmarchive.com

This diary has been reprinted in facsimile from the original. Any imperfections are inevitably reproduced and the quality may fall short of modern type and cartographic standards.

© **Crown Copyright**
Images reproduced by permission of The National Archives, London, England, 2015.

Contents

Document type	Place/Title	Date From	Date To
Heading	WO95/2816/2		
Heading	D.A. Dir. Ordnance Services Apr 1915-May 1919		
Heading	D A D O S 50th Division April & May 1915		
War Diary		19/04/1915	30/04/1915
War Diary		01/05/1915	31/05/1915
Heading	50th Division D A D O S 50th Division Vol I June 1915		
War Diary		01/06/1915	30/06/1915
Heading	D A D O S 50th Division Vol II July 1915		
Heading	War Diary Of D.A.D.O.S. Of 50th Division From 1.7.15 To 31.7.15		
War Diary		01/07/1915	31/07/1915
Heading	50th Division D A D O S 50th Division Vol III August 15		
Heading	War Diary Of D.A.D.O.S. 50th Division From 1.8.15 To 31.8.15		
War Diary	Pont-De-Nieppe	01/08/1915	31/08/1915
Heading	50th Division D A D O S 50th Division Vol IV Sept 15		
Heading	War Diary Of D.A.D.O.S. 50th Division 1.9.15 to 30.9.15		
War Diary	Pont-De-Nieppe	01/09/1915	30/09/1915
Heading	War Diary Of D.A.D.O.S. 50th Division 1-31.10.15 Vol V		
War Diary	Pont-De-Nieppe	01/11/1915	01/11/1915
War Diary	Pont-De-Nieppe	01/10/1915	31/10/1915
Heading	D.A.D.O.S. 50th Divn Nov 1915		
Miscellaneous	Major A Gibson Major D.A.D.O.S. 50th (Northb'n) Division		
War Diary	Pont-De-Nieppe	01/11/1915	09/11/1915
War Diary	Merris	10/11/1915	30/11/1915
Heading	D A D O S 50th Div Dec Vol VII		
Miscellaneous	Major A A Gibson D A D O S 50th Division		
War Diary	Merris	01/12/1915	20/12/1915
War Diary	Poperinghe	20/12/1915	31/12/1915
Heading	D A D O S 50th Div Jan Vol VIII		
Miscellaneous	Lieutenant A.A Roth A.O.D D.A.D.O.S. 50th Division		
War Diary	Poperinghe	01/01/1916	31/01/1916
Heading	Lieut A A Roth A O D D A D O S 50th Division February 1915 Vol IX		
War Diary	Poperinghe	01/02/1916	29/02/1916
War Diary	Domart	01/03/1916	11/03/1916
War Diary	Douthans	12/03/1916	13/03/1916
War Diary	Le Cauroy	14/03/1916	31/03/1916
Heading	D.A.D.O.S. 50 Div Vol X		
Heading	D A D O S 50th Division A A Roth Capt April 1916		
War Diary	Westoutre	01/04/1916	26/04/1916
War Diary	Fletre	27/04/1916	30/04/1916
War Diary	Westoutre	28/04/1916	30/04/1916
Heading	June 1916 Captain A A Roth A O D D A D O S 50th Division		

War Diary	Westoutre	01/06/1916	30/06/1916
Heading	Capt A.A. Roth A.O.D. D.A.D.O.S. July 1916 50th Division Volume 16		
War Diary	Westoutre	01/07/1916	31/07/1916
Heading	D.A.D.O.S. 50th Division August 1916		
War Diary	Fletre	01/08/1916	17/08/1916
War Diary	Montigny	18/08/1916	31/08/1916
Heading	Capt A A. Roth D.A.D.O.S. 50th Divn September 1916		
War Diary	Montigny	01/09/1916	09/09/1916
War Diary	Near Millencourt	10/09/1916	15/09/1916
War Diary	Somme	16/09/1916	20/09/1916
War Diary	Near Millencourt	21/09/1916	30/09/1916
Heading	War Diary Of D.A.D.O.S. 50th Division From 1st October 1916 to 31st October 1916		
War Diary	Near Millencourt Hude Cannos	01/10/1916	20/10/1916
War Diary	Near Millencourt	21/10/1916	24/10/1916
War Diary	Near Fricourt Hinder Cannon	25/10/1916	31/10/1916
Heading	Capt. A.A. Roth D.A.D.O.S. 50th Division November 1916		
War Diary	Near Fricourt Hunde Cannas	01/11/1916	30/11/1916
Heading	Capt A.A. Roth D A D O S 50th Divn December 1916		
War Diary	Baizient Somme	01/12/1916	14/12/1916
War Diary	Bazieux	15/12/1916	31/12/1916
Heading	War Diary D.A.D.O.S. 50th Division From 1-31st January 1917		
Heading	Capt A.A. Roth A.O.D. DADOS 50th Divn January 1917		
War Diary	Albert Somme	01/01/1917	31/01/1917
Heading	Capt A A Roth A.O.D. DADOS 50th Divn February 1917		
War Diary	Albert Ribemont	01/02/1917	13/02/1917
War Diary	Proyart	14/02/1917	22/02/1917
Heading	Captain A.A. Roth A.O.D DADOS 50th Division March 1917		
War Diary	Proyart	01/03/1917	04/03/1917
War Diary	Mericourt Sur Somme	09/03/1917	31/03/1917
Heading	Capt. A.A. Roth A.O.D. DADOS 50th Division April 1917		
War Diary	Molliens Au Bois	01/04/1917	04/04/1917
War Diary	Givenchy Le Noble	05/04/1917	11/04/1917
War Diary	Arras	12/04/1917	26/04/1917
War Diary	Couturelle	27/04/1917	29/04/1917
Heading	Capt A. A. Roth A.O.D DADOS 50th Division May 1917		
War Diary	Couturelle	01/05/1917	01/05/1917
War Diary	Basseux	02/05/1917	04/05/1917
War Diary	Couturelle	07/05/1917	24/05/1917
War Diary	Capt A A Roth D A D O S 50th Divn June 1917		
War Diary	Couin	01/06/1917	17/06/1917
War Diary	Boisleaux Au Mont	18/06/1917	29/06/1917
Heading	Capt A A Roth D A D O S July 1917 50th		
War Diary	Boisleux Au Mont	03/07/1917	29/07/1917
Heading	Capt A A Roth D A D O S 50th Divn August 1917		
War Diary	Boisleaux Au Mont	02/08/1917	28/08/1917
Heading	Capt A A Roth D A D O S 50th Divn September 1917		
War Diary	Boisleaux Au Mont	02/09/1917	27/09/1917

Heading	Capt A A Roth D A D O S 50th Division October 1917		
War Diary	Boileux Au Mont	03/10/1917	12/10/1917
War Diary	Achiet Le Petit	15/10/1917	15/10/1917
War Diary	Lederzeele	16/10/1917	20/10/1917
War Diary	Proven	22/10/1917	23/10/1917
War Diary	Elverdinghe	24/10/1917	29/10/1917
Heading	Capt A A Roth D A D O S 50th Division November 1917		
War Diary	Elverdinghe	01/11/1917	10/11/1917
War Diary	Epilecques	11/11/1917	30/11/1917
Heading	Capt A A Roth D A D O S 50th Division December 1917		
War Diary	Epislecques	02/12/1917	13/12/1917
War Diary	Brandhoek	14/12/1917	23/12/1917
Heading	War Diary Of A.D. Of V.S. 50th Division From 1.1.17 to 31.1.17		
Heading	Captain A A Roth DADOS 50 Division January 1918		
War Diary	Brandhoek	01/01/1918	18/01/1918
War Diary	Wizernes	19/01/1918	29/01/1918
War Diary	Brandhoek	30/01/1918	31/01/1918
Heading	Capt A A Roth DADOS 50th Division February 18		
War Diary	Brandhoek	01/02/1918	28/02/1918
Heading	Capt A A Roth DADOS 50th Divn March 1918		
War Diary	Wizernes	01/03/1918	09/03/1918
War Diary	Montaul	10/03/1918	10/03/1918
War Diary	Harbonniers	14/03/1918	31/03/1918
Heading	Volume 37 Capt. A.A. Roth DADOS 50th Division April 1918		
War Diary	Douriez	01/04/1918	01/04/1918
War Diary	Robecq	05/04/1918	08/04/1918
War Diary	Merville	09/04/1918	13/04/1918
War Diary	Wittes	15/04/1918	30/04/1918
Heading	Capt A.A. Roth D.A.D.O.S. 50th Division May 1918		
War Diary	Beaurieux	01/05/1918	31/05/1918
Heading	Capt A.A. Roth DADOS 50th Vol 39		
War Diary	Vert La Gravell	01/06/1918	09/06/1918
War Diary	Mondement	10/06/1918	17/06/1918
War Diary	Beauvais	18/06/1918	30/06/1918
Heading	Volume 40 Major A A Roth DADOS 50th Division For July 1918		
War Diary	Supply	01/07/1918	14/07/1918
War Diary	Marlins Eglise	15/07/1918	31/07/1918
Heading	War Diary Major A A Roth DADOS 50th Division August 1918		
War Diary	Martin Eglise	01/08/1918	31/08/1918
Heading	Volume No 43 Major A A Roth A.O.D. DADOS 50th Division		
War Diary	Martin Eglise	01/08/1918	15/08/1918
War Diary	Lucheux	16/08/1918	21/08/1918
War Diary	Montigny	26/08/1918	26/08/1918
War Diary	Combles	28/08/1918	30/08/1918
Heading	Diary Of Major A A Roth DADOS 50th Division For October		
War Diary	Lieramont	01/10/1918	05/10/1918
War Diary	Epiphy	06/10/1918	12/10/1918
War Diary	Goyancourt Farm	14/10/1918	14/10/1918

War Diary	La Laux Aux Soldats	14/10/1918	31/10/1918
Heading	Diary Of Major A A Roth DADOS 50th Division November 1918		
War Diary	La Coisax	01/11/1918	07/11/1918
War Diary	Fontove Lon Bois	08/11/1918	09/11/1918
War Diary	Perfelles	09/11/1918	10/11/1918
War Diary	Doullens	11/11/1918	30/11/1918
Heading	Royal Army Ordnance Corps Major A.A. Roth R.A.O.C., O.B.E. (M) December 1918 Volume 46		
War Diary	Dourlers.	01/12/1918	19/12/1918
War Diary	Le Quisex	19/12/1918	31/12/1918
Heading	Royal Army Ordnance Corps January 1919 Major A.A. Roth OBE RAOC D.A.D.O.S. 50th Division Volume 47		
War Diary	Le Quesnoy	01/01/1919	31/01/1919
Heading	Royal Army Ordnance Corps Major A.A. Roth O.B.E. February 1919 Volume 48		
War Diary	Le Quesnoy	01/02/1919	28/02/1919
Heading	Royal Army Ordnance Corps Major A.A. Roth March 1919 Volume 49		
War Diary	Le Quesnoy	01/03/1919	31/03/1919
Heading	Royal Army Ordnance Corps Lieut., F.A.E. Pine April 1919 Volume 50		
War Diary	Le Quesnoy	01/04/1919	29/04/1919
Heading	Royal Army Ordnance Corps Lieut F.A.E. Pine O.O. I.C.S. Landrecies May 1919 Volume 51		
War Diary	Le Quesnoy	01/05/1919	14/05/1919
War Diary	Landrears	15/05/1919	30/05/1919

WD95/2816/2

50TH DIVISION

D.A.DIR. ORDNANCE SERVICES

APR 1915-MAY 1919

DADOS

50th Division

April + May

1915

Confidential   **April**
British Expeditionary Force / France

Diary of D.A.D.O.S. 50th (North'n) Division. J.F.

19/4/15	Left Newcastle-on-Tyne on Monday 19th April. Arrived at Havre on the 21st and proceeded to Steenvoorde arriving there on the evening of 23rd inst.
24/4	Secured a dump and arranged with Divisional supply officer for 4. 3 ton motor trolleys.
25/4	Visited surrounding districts to ascertain local resources. Very few useful stores left except wood (ash) obtainable in small quantities suitable for repairing vehicles. The French & Belgian Governments have bought up nearly everything and most of the work shops here are under Government control.
26/4	First consignment of stores arrived for Division. I visited Railhead and superintended the collection and despatch.

Confd'tl April Cont'd

27/4/15   Visited Railhead superintended collection and despatch of stores

28/4/15   Visited Brigades and refilling Depôts in connection with the distribution of stores, general Office work.

29/4/15   Visited Railhead superintended distribution and despatch of stores and general office work

30/4/15   General Routine duties

Gibson Major
D.A.D.O.S.
50th Division

May 4 Sheets   No 1

Confidential

British Expedy Force. France

Diary of D.A.D.O.S. 50th (Northb) Division

1 - 5/15 Proceeded to Railhead to superintend distribution and despatch of stores — General Office work

One of our trolleys was damaged by German shell fire while delivering stores near Ypres. The W O in charge was slightly wounded.

2 5/15 Proceeded to Railhead to superintend distribution and despatch of stores. General Office work

3 5/15 General Routine work.

4 5/15 ———— Do ————

5 5/15 ———— Do ————

6 5/15 ———— Do ————

A number of Shovels, accoutrements, etc found. Collected & returned to Base

Confidential   May Cont'd   No 7

4 5/15   Visited Railhead, superintended
          distribution and despatch of stores.
          General Office work.

8 5/15   General Routine work.

9 5/15   General Routine work.

10 5/15 General Routine work.

11 5/15 General Routine work.

12 5/15 General Routine work.

13 5/15 General Routine work.

14 5/15 General Routine work.

15 5/15 General Routine work.

16 5/15 General Routine work

17 5/15 Division moved to Poperinghe
          Ordnance Dump and Office
          Shelled on day of arrival there

Norfolks   May Cont'd   No 3

17/5/15   Stores removed out of range
of shell fire without casualties

18/5/15   Visited Railhead superintended
distribution and despatch of
stores.

19/5/15   General Routine Work

20/5/15   General Routine Work

21/5/15   General Routine work.

22/5/15   General Routine work

23/5/15   General Routine work.

24/5/15   General Routine work

25/5/15   Division transferred to
Watacu. Fresh dump
formed.

26/5/15   General Routine work.

27/5/15   General Routine work.

Confidl May Cont'd No 4

28 5/15 General Routine work.

29 5/15 General Routine work.

30 5/15 General Routine work.

31 5/15 General Routine work.
Collected large quantity of abandoned stores near Ypres and returned them to Base

A. Robson Major
ADSS
50th Division

121/6033

50th Division

DADOS. 50th Division
Vol I
June 1915

Confid^l   3 sheets   No 1
June

British Expeditionary Force France

Diary of DADOS 50th (Northb^d) Divⁿ

1/6/15.   Division transferred from
          Watou to Abeele District
          Fresh dump formed in small
          ~~barn~~ barn.

2/6/15.   Visited Railhead, superintended
          distribution and despatch of
          ~~stores~~ stores. General office work.

3/6/15   General Routine Work

4/6/15   General Routine Work

5/6/15   Division transferred from
          Abeele District to Brassboom
          Fresh dump formed.

6/6/15   General Routine Work

7/6/15   General Routine work abandoned
          Collected a large quantity of stores
          near Ypres consisting of Arms, Unser machine
          Gun, 2 water carts accts etc

Carfath   June Cont'd   Nov

8 6/15   General Routine Work
9 6/15   General Routine work
10 6/15   General Routine work
11 6/15   General Routine work
12 6/15   General Routine work
13 6/15   General Routine work
14 6/15   General Routine work
15 6/15   General Routine work
16 6/15   General Routine work
17 6/15   General Routine work
18 6/15   General Routine work
19 6/15   General Routine work
20 6/15   General Routine work

June cont'd   No 3

21/6/15   General Routine Work
22/6/15   General Routine work
23/6/15   General Routine work
24/6/15   Division transferred from Boesboom to Bailleul. Fresh dump formed.
25/6/15   General Routine work.
26/6/15   General Routine work
27/6/15   General Routine work.
28/6/15   General Routine work.
29/6/15   General Routine work
30/6/15   General Routine work

                    Gibson Major
                    D.A.D.O.S.
                    56th Division

121/6390

50th Division

DADOS. 50th Division

Vol II

July 1915

Army Form C. 2118.

WAR DIARY
INTELLIGENCE SUMMARY.
(Erase heading not required.)

Instructions regarding War Diaries and Intelligence Summaries are contained in F.S. Regs., Part II. and the Staff Manual respectively. Title pages will be prepared in manuscript.

Hour, Date, Place	Summary of Events and Information	Remarks and references to Appendices
	Confidential. War Diary of:- D.A.D. of 50th Division. (Major A. Gibson. A.O.D.) From: 1. 7. 15. To 31. 7. 15.	

(73989) W4141—463. 400,000. 9/14. H.&J.Ltd. Forms/C. 2118/10.

July 1915

Head Quarters
50th (Northbr) Division
British Exped'y Force.
France

Diary of D.A.D.O.S.

1/7/15 Visited Railhead, superintended distribution and despatch of stores. General Office work.

2/7/15 General Routine work.

3/7/15 General Routine work.

4/7/15 General Routine work

5/7/15 General Routine work

6/7/15 General Routine work

7/7/15 General Routine work

8/7/15 General Routine work

9/7/15 General Routine work.

July Cont'd

10/7/15	General Routine Work
11/7/15	General Routine Work
12/7/15	General Routine work
13/7/15	General Routine work
14/7/15	General Routine work
15/7/15	General Routine work
16/7/15	General Routine work
17/7/15	General Routine work
18/7/15	General Routine work
19/7/15	General Routine work
20/7/15	Moved from Bailleul to Nieppe
21/7/15	General Routine work
22/7/15	General Routine work

July Cont'd.

23/7/15   General Routine Work
          Local supply of timber
          for repairs good.

24/7/15   General Routine work.

25/7/15   General Routine work.

26/7/15   General Routine work.

27/7/15   General Routine work.

28/7/15   General Routine work.

29/7/15   General Routine work.

30/7/15   General Routine work.

31/7/15   General Routine work.

                    Gibson Major
                    DADOS
                    56th Div'n

121/6802

DOS.

50th Division

DADOS. 50th Division

Stat

August 15

Army Form C. 2118.

WAR DIARY
INTELLIGENCE SUMMARY.
(Erase heading not required.)

Instructions regarding War Diaries and Intelligence Summaries are contained in F. S. Regs., Part II. and the Staff Manual respectively. Title pages will be prepared in manuscript.

Hour, Date, Place	Summary of Events and Information	Remarks and references to Appendices
	Confidential. War Diary of: D.A.D.O.S. 50th Division (Major A. G. ibson aon.) From: 1-8-15. To:- 31-8-15.	

Confidential Sheet 1

Head Quarters,
50th Division,
B. E. Force
France

Army Form C. 2118
(2 sheets)

WAR DIARY
or
INTELLIGENCE SUMMARY

(Erase heading not required.)

Instructions regarding War Diaries and Intelligence Summaries are contained in F. S. Regs., Part II and the Staff Manual respectively. Title Pages will be prepared in manuscript.

Place	Date	Hour	Summary of Events and Information	Remarks and references to Appendices
Pont-de-Nieppe	1-8-15		August 1915	
			Visited Railhead, superintended distribution and despatch of stores. General Office work	
	2-8		General Routine work	
	3-8		General Routine work	
	4-8		General Routine work	
	5-8		General Routine work	
	6-8		General Routine work	
	7-8		General Routine work	
	8-8		General Routine work	
	9-8		General Routine work	
	10-8		General Routine work	
	11-8		General Routine work	
	12-8		General Routine work	
	13-8		General Routine work	
	14-8		General Routine work	
	15-8		General Routine work	
	16-8		General Routine work	
	17-8		General Routine work	
	18-8		General Routine work	
	19-8		General Routine work	
	20-8		General Routine work	
	21-8		General Routine work	

Confidential

Army Form C. 2118

Head Quarters Sheet
50th Division
B.E.F. France

WAR DIARY
or
INTELLIGENCE SUMMARY
(Erase heading not required.)

Instructions regarding War Diaries and Intelligence Summaries are contained in F. S. Regs., Part II. and the Staff Manual respectively. Title Pages will be prepared in manuscript.

Place	Date	Hour	Summary of Events and Information	Remarks and references to Appendices
Pont-de-Nieppe			August 1915	
	22-8		General Routine work	
	23-8		General Routine work	
	24-8		General Routine work	
	25-8		General Routine work	
	26-8		General Routine work	
	27-8		General Routine work	
	28-8		General Routine work	
	29-8		General Routine work	
	30-8		General Routine work	
	31-8		General Routine work	

Wilson Major
D.A.D.S.
50th Division

121/6971

50th Division

DADOS. 50th Division

Vol IV

Sept. 15

Army Form C. 2118.

WAR DIARY
of
INTELLIGENCE SUMMARY.
(Erase heading not required.)

Instructions regarding War Diaries and Intelligence Summaries are contained in F. S. Regs., Part II. and the Staff Manual respectively. Title pages will be prepared in manuscript.

Hour, Date, Place	Summary of Events and Information	Remarks and references to Appendices
	Confidential War Diary of D.A.D.O.S. 50th Division (Major A.A.Gibson) 1-9-15. To 30-9-15.	

[Stamp: A.L.C. AT THE BASE — 4 OCT 1915 — W.O.O. SECTION]

Confidential

Major A. Hilgson,
D.A.D.V.S.
56th Division.
D.E. Force,
France.

Sheet 1.
Army Form C. 2118
(3 sheets)

WAR DIARY
or
INTELLIGENCE SUMMARY
(Erase heading not required.)

Instructions regarding War Diaries and Intelligence Summaries are contained in F. S. Regs., Part II. and the Staff Manual respectively. Title Pages will be prepared in manuscript.

Place	Date	Hour	Summary of Events and Information	Remarks and references to Appendices
Pont-de-Fieppe	1/9/15		General Routine work, September 1915 AH	
	2/9		General Routine work	AH
	3/9		A Divisional Blacksmiths shop opened for remaking old horse shoes. The necessary staff has been drawn from mounted Units in Division. This shop is under the supervision of the A.D.V.S.	AH
	4/9		General Routine work	AH
	5/9		General Routine work	AH
	6/9		General Routine work	AH
	7/9		General Routine work	AH
	8/9		General Routine work	AH
	9/9		General Routine work	AH
	10/9		General Routine work	AH
	11/9		General Routine work	AH
	12/9		General Routine work	AH
	13/9		General Routine work	AH
	14/9		A Divisional Bootrepairing shop opened under my supervision. The staff consisting of 1 Sergt and 6 men have been drawn from	AH

Confidential

Major A. Gibson
D.A.D.O.S.
50th Division

Army Form C. 2118
Sheet 2

WAR DIARY
or
INTELLIGENCE SUMMARY
(Erase heading not required.)

Instructions regarding War Diaries and Intelligence Summaries are contained in F.S. Regs., Part II. and the Staff Manual respectively. Title Pages will be prepared in manuscript.

Place	Date	Hour	Summary of Events and Information	Remarks and references to Appendices
Pont-de-Nieppe	15/9 – 14/9		From the various Infantry Units in the Division. All old boots beyond repair regimentally are sent here for repair, also those collected by the Salvage Corps from vacated billets and camps. These boots after repair and a liberal dressing of dubbing are handed into the A.O.D. dump and re-issued. It is anticipated that a considerable saving will be effected by the opening of this shop.	AG AG AG AG AG AG AG AG AG AG
	15/9		General Routine work.	
	16/9		General Routine work.	
	17/9		General Routine work.	
	18/9		General Routine work.	
	19/9		General Routine work.	
	20/9		General Routine work.	
	21/9		General Routine work.	
	22/9		General Routine work.	
	23/9		General Routine work.	
	24/9		General Routine work.	

Sheet 3
Army Form C.2118

Confidential

WAR DIARY
or
INTELLIGENCE SUMMARY

(Erase heading not required.)

Instructions regarding War Diaries and Intelligence Summaries are contained in F. S. Regs., Part II. and the Staff Manual respectively. Title Pages will be prepared in manuscript.

Place	Date	Hour	Summary of Events and Information	Remarks and references to Appendices
Pont-de-Nieppe	25/9		Divisional Blacksmiths shop partly destroyed by shell fire. Two casualties. Shop closed temporarily	
	26/9		General Routine work.	
	27/9		General Routine work.	
	28/9		General Routine work.	
	29/9		General Routine work	
	30/9		General Routine work	

Wilson Major
A.D.S.S.
50th Division

121/7449

War Diary
of
D.A.D.O. of
50th Division
(Major Gibson and
-1-31 10/15 - Vol V

Army Form C. 2118

WAR DIARY
INTELLIGENCE SUMMARY
(Erase heading not required.)

Confidential

October 1915

Major A. Hilson
D.A.D.O.S.
50th Division

Place	Date	Hour	Summary of Events and Information	Remarks and references to Appendices
Port-de-Trappe	1/15			

Confidential

Major A. Gibson 2 Sheets
D.A.D.S.
5 & 5 Division No. 7.

WAR DIARY
or
INTELLIGENCE SUMMARY

Army Form C. 2118

Instructions regarding War Diaries and Intelligence Summaries are contained in F. S. Regs., Part II. and the Staff Manual respectively. Title Pages will be prepared in manuscript.

Place	Date	Hour	Summary of Events and Information	Remarks and references to Appendices
Pont-de-Nieppe	1/10/15		October 1915	
			General Routine work.	
	2/10		General Routine work.	
	3/10		General Routine work.	
	4/10		General Routine work.	
	5/10		General Routine work.	
	6/10		General Routine work.	
	7/10		General Routine work.	
	8/10		General Routine work.	
	9/10		General Routine work.	
	10/10		General Routine work.	
	11/10		General Routine work.	
	12/10		General Routine work.	
	13/10		General Routine work.	
	14/10		General Routine work.	
	15/10		General Routine work.	
	16/10		General Routine work.	
	17/10		General Routine work.	
	18/10		General Routine work.	

Confidential

Army Form C. 2118

WAR DIARY
or
INTELLIGENCE SUMMARY

(Erase heading not required.)

Place	Date	Hour	Summary of Events and Information	Remarks and references to Appendices
Pont-de-Nieppe	19/10		General Routine work	
	20/10		General Routine work	
	21/10		General Routine work	
	22/10		General Routine work	
	23/10		General Routine work	
	24/10		General Routine work	
	25/10		General Routine work	
	26/10		General Routine work	
	27/10		General Routine work	
	28/10		General Routine work	
	29/10		General Routine work	
	30/10		General Routine work	
	31/10		General Routine work	

J. H. Gibson
Major
D.A.D.O.S.
50th Division

121/7603

D.A.D.O.S. 50th Divn.

N 2nd Sigs

Vol VI

WAR DIARY
or
INTELLIGENCE SUMMARY

Army Form C. 2118

Major A. Wilson, Major,
D.A.D.S.
58th (Northern) Division

Army Form C. 2118
Sheet No 7

WAR DIARY
or
INTELLIGENCE SUMMARY
(Erase heading not required.)

2 Sheet

Instructions regarding War Diaries and Intelligence Summaries are contained in F. S. Regs., Part II. and the Staff Manual respectively. Title Pages will be prepared in manuscript.

Place	Date 1915	Hour	Summary of Events and Information	Remarks and references to Appendices
Pont-de-Nieppe	1/11	―	General routine work.	
" "	2/11	―	General routine work.	
" "	3/11	―	General routine work.	
" "	4/11	―	General routine work.	
" "	5/11	―	General routine work.	
" "	6/11	―	General routine work.	
" "	7/11	―	General routine work.	
" "	8/11	―	General routine work.	
" "	9/11		General routine work.	
Meris	10/11		Moved to Meris, a small village of 1000 inhabitants. Very hard work in connection with reception & issue of Winter clothing.	
" "	11/11		General routine work.	
" "	12/11		General routine work.	
" "	13/11		General routine work.	
" "	14/11		General routine work.	
" "	15/11		General routine work.	
" "	16/11		General routine work.	
" "	17/11		General routine work.	
" "	18/11		General routine work.	
" "	19/11		General routine work.	
" "	20/11		General routine work.	

A. Gibson Major
D.A.D.O.S.
50th Division

Army Form C. 2118

Sheet No 2

WAR DIARY
or
INTELLIGENCE SUMMARY
(Erase heading not required.)

Place	Date 1915	Hour	Summary of Events and Information	Remarks and references to Appendices
Merris	21/11		General routine work. AG	
"	22/11		General routine work. AG	
"	23/11		General routine work. AG	
"	24/11		General routine work. AG	
"	25/11		General routine work. AG	
"	26/11		General routine work. AG	
"	27/11		General routine work. AG	
"	28/11		General routine work. AG	
"	29/11		General routine work. AG	
"	30/11		General routine work. AG	

A. Wilson Major
D.A.D.S.
5 Div Div'n

DADOS 50 a.
Dez
vol. VII

Confidential
Army Form C. 2118

WAR DIARY
or
INTELLIGENCE SUMMARY

(Erase heading not required.)

December 1915

Instructions regarding War Diaries and Intelligence Summaries are contained in F. S. Regs., Part II. and the Staff Manual respectively. Title Pages will be prepared in manuscript.

Place	Date	Hour	Summary of Events and Information	Remarks and references to Appendices

Major A.A. Gibson
D.A.D.S.
50th Division

The Officer i/c Adjutant General's Office,
Base

Confidential

Major A.H. Wilson
SS & 5O Division

WAR DIARY
of
INTELLIGENCE SUMMARY
(Erase heading not required.)

Army Form C. 2118

Instructions regarding War Diaries and Intelligence Summaries are contained in F. S. Regs., Part II. and the Staff Manual respectively. Title Pages will be prepared in manuscript.

Place	Date	Hour	Summary of Events and Information	Remarks and references to Appendices
Menio	1/12/15		General routine work	
"	2/12		General routine work	
"	3/12		General routine work	
"	4/12		General routine work	
"	5/12		General routine work	
"	6/12		General routine work	
"	7/12		General routine work	
"	8/12		General routine work	
"	9/12		General routine work	
"	10/12		General routine work	
"	11/12		General routine work	
"	13/12		General routine work	
"	14/12		General routine work	
"	15/12		General routine work	
"	16/12		General routine work	
"	17/12		General routine work	
"	18/12		General routine work	

Confidential

Army Form C. 2118

WAR DIARY
~~INTELLIGENCE SUMMARY~~ December
(Erase heading not required.)

Instructions regarding War Diaries and Intelligence Summaries are contained in F. S. Regs., Part II. and the Staff Manual respectively. Title Pages will be prepared in manuscript.

Place	Date 1915	Hour	Summary of Events and Information	Remarks and references to Appendices
Mervio	19/12		General routine work.	
"	30/12		Ordered to Marseilles for duty elsewhere.	

A. Gibson major
D.A.D.S.C.
50th Division

WAR DIARY
or
INTELLIGENCE SUMMARY
(Erase heading not required.)

Army Form C. 2118

Place	Date 1912	Hour	Summary of Events and Information	Remarks and references to Appendices
Poperinghe	20/12		Arrived here from Merris. Succeeded Major Gibson as D.A.D.O.S. of the division. Arranged with D.A.D.O.S. 9th Division to leave the reserve of Ordinary Arms & Helmets 15, 2470 at Merris & for him to leave his reserve at Poperinghe in order to save unnecessary transferring items. General Routine work	
	21 22 23 24 25 26		General Routine work	
	27		The necessity of gum boots for this part of the line both for transport men as well as those in the trenches very marked, by the continual demand for them from unit units.	
	28 29 30 31		Supply of woollen vests, khaki helmets (anti-gas) very much improved. General Routine work	

A. J. Rott, Lieut D.A.D.O.S.

Army Form C. 2118

WAR DIARY
Confidential
or
INTELLIGENCE SUMMARY

December 20th to 31st 1915

(Erase heading not required.)

Lieut. A. A. Roth.
D.A.D.O.S
50th Division

DADOS 50 in Dn / Jan / Vol VIII

Army Form C. 2118

WAR DIARY
or
INTELLIGENCE SUMMARY

(Erase heading not required.)

Confidential   January 1 - 31st 1916

Place	Date	Hour	Summary of Events and Information	Remarks and references to Appendices
			Lieutenant A. A. Roth. A.O.D D.A.D.O.S. 58th Division	

Army Form C. 2118

WAR DIARY
or
INTELLIGENCE SUMMARY
(Erase heading not required.)

Instructions regarding War Diaries and Intelligence Summaries are contained in F. S. Regs., Part II. and the Staff Manual respectively. Title Pages will be prepared in manuscript.

Place	Date	Hour	Summary of Events and Information	Remarks and references to Appendices
Paperinghe	1916 January			
	1		General Routine	
	2			
	3			
	4			
	5			
	6			
	7			
	8			
	9			
	10			
	11			
	12			
	13			
	14		51 heavy Guns arrived from France to replace Machine Guns transferred for use with Machine Gun Corps	
	15			
	16		8 4.5 Howitzers arrived to replace 5 for the 4th Northumbrian Howitzer Bde	
	17		General Routine	
	18-26		C.O. Helped begin to arrive for tou officers	
	27		General Routine	
	28-31			

A.J. Fisk N
? A.D. OS
50th Div

Army Form C. 2118

WAR DIARY
or
INTELLIGENCE SUMMARY
(Erase heading not required.)

Lieut A N Rok. A.D.O
PADUS
50th Division

February 1915
Vol IX

Army Form C. 2118

WAR DIARY
or
INTELLIGENCE SUMMARY
(Erase heading not required.)

February 1916

Instructions regarding War Diaries and Intelligence Summaries are contained in F. S. Regs., Part II. and the Staff Manual respectively. Title Pages will be prepared in manuscript.

Place	Date	Hour	Summary of Events and Information	Remarks and references to Appendices
Poperinghe	1			
	2			
	3			
	4			
	5			
	6			
	7			
	8			
	9			
	10			
	11			
	12			
	13			
	14			
	15			
	16			
	17			
	18		General Ainslie	
	19			
	20			
	21			
	22			
	23			
	24		Completed the issue of F.H. Helmets 2 per Officer & man.	
	25		General Ainslie	
	26			
	27			
	28			
	29			

1875 W¹. W 593/826 1,000,000 4/15 J.B.C. & A. A.D.S.S./Forms/C. 2118.

Army Form C. 2118.

WAR DIARY
INTELLIGENCE SUMMARY.
(Erase heading not required.)

Instructions regarding War Diaries and Intelligence Summaries are contained in F. S. Regs., Part II. and the Staff Manual respectively. Title pages will be prepared in manuscript.

Place	Date	Hour	Summary of Events and Information	Remarks and references to Appendices
Bonart	1/3/16		Proceeded to Hallencourt in connection with removal of Reserves.	
	2/3		Established Dump for convenience of Troops drawing skins at Bonu Le Petite. The 4 Lorries for use of B.O.S. received from Civil Supply Columns were handed over to they.	
	3/3			
	4/3	}	General Routine duties. Stores are coming up from base in very large quantities	
	5/3			
	6/3		Dumps removed from La Petite to Bonart.	
	7/3		Ordered to proceed to hanieres for duty	
	8/			

[signature]
D.A.D.S.S
58 Div

Army Form C. 2118.

WAR DIARY
or
INTELLIGENCE SUMMARY
(Erase heading not required.)

Instructions regarding War Diaries and Intelligence
Summaries are contained in F.S. Regs., Part II.
and the Staff Manual respectively. Title pages
will be prepared in manuscript.

Place	Date	Hour	Summary of Events and Information	Remarks and references to Appendices
Domart	8/3/16		Major Bishop proceeded to Marieux for duty. Temp. Lieut. Little took over duties. Graded J to D.A.D.V.S.	A.1.
	9/3/16		Departmental duties. Received 26 Lewis guns for distribution	A.1
	10/3/16		Received 14700 P.H. smoke helmets. Arranged with A.D.M.S. as to distribution.	A.1.
	11/5/16		Received orders to move to Doullens on 12th. Moved to Doullens 10 p.m. a suitable dump	A.1
Doullens	12/3/16		Moved to Doullens. Radlhum changed form Cavalry to Divisional. Received 40 Vickers guns for machine gun companies.	A.2
	13/3/16		Colonel Moulton Barrett visited Advance Dump. Had interviews from to Le Cauroy.	A.2
Le Cauroy	14/3/16		Moved to Le Cauroy. Owing to accumulation gates including Vickers gun & P.H. Smoke helmets, nineteen lorry loads were transported. Dump chosen for use in mud unsatisfactory.	A.3
"	15/3/16		Whole day required in moving to a new dump owing to the one found for use not being suitable.	A.1.
"	16/3/16		Departmental Duties	A.1

Army Form C. 2118.

WAR DIARY
or
INTELLIGENCE SUMMARY.
(Erase heading not required.)

Instructions regarding War Diaries and Intelligence Summaries are contained in F. S. Regs., Part II. and the Staff Manual respectively. Title pages will be prepared in manuscript.

Place	Date	Hour	Summary of Events and Information	Remarks and references to Appendices
Le Cauroy	17/3/16		Visited by A.D.V.S. 6th Corps. Inspn of P.H. Kdruds & Division begun. Visitors from reinov to 167th 168th & 169th Brigades.	P.1.
"	18/3/16		Departmental duties	P.1.
"	19/3/16		Visited by A.D.V.S. 6th Corps. Departmental duties.	P.1.
"	20/3/16		Went to Bryant Lves 1/4 London Regt & then team given who visits A.V.C. 6th Corps at Izydole-Vion	P.1.
"	21/3/16		Departmental duties	P.1.
"	22/3/16		"	P.1.
"	23/3/16		Went to Doullens. Made local purchases.	P.1.
"	24/3/16		Departmental duties.	P.1.
"	25/3/16		Visited by A.D.V.S. 6th Corps. Returned on tour for second issue of P.H. Helmets to Div.	P.2.
"	26/3/16		Departmental duties	P.1.
"	27/3/16		Went to Harbang. Looked bulges 17th from D.A.V.S. 5th Div. Dillos re A.D.V.S. 6th Corps	P.1.
"	28/3/16		Received 15870 "P.H." tube Helmets hospital Division to have Helmets for man	P.2.
"	29/3/16		Went to Bouvain Abordeau. chairs for Divisional school	P.1.
"	30/3/16		Departmental duties	P.1.

F.J. Libby
D.A.V.S. 5th Div.

D. A. D. O. S. 50 Div
Vol X

WAR DIARY or INTELLIGENCE SUMMARY

Army Form C. 2118

D.A.D.O.S.
50th Division

Vol XI

A.D.S. Roth
Capt

April 1916

Army Form C. 2118

WAR DIARY
or
INTELLIGENCE SUMMARY
(Erase heading not required.)

Instructions regarding War Diaries and Intelligence Summaries are contained in F. S. Regs., Part II. and the Staff Manual respectively. Title Pages will be prepared in manuscript.

Place	Date	Hour	Summary of Events and Information	Remarks and references to Appendices
Meteren	1–15		General Routine.	
	16		Return of Winter clothing proceeding satisfactorily.	
	17		1 Lewis gun received & replaces one damaged by shell fire. 5th Border Regt.	
	18		Visited all Brigades	
	19		— CRA + DAC	
	20		— all Field Ambulances	
	23		one Lewis gun received to replace one condemned by armourer 4th Yorks Regt.	
	24–26		General Routine	
Flêtre	27–30		General Routine	

1875 Wt. W593/826 1,000,000 4/15 J.B.C. & A. A.D.S.S./Forms/C. 2118.

Army Form C. 2118

WAR DIARY
or
INTELLIGENCE SUMMARY
(Erase heading not required.)

Capt. [signature]
DADOS
50th Divn
May 1916.

1st 12

WAR DIARY
or
INTELLIGENCE SUMMARY

(Erase heading not required.)

Army Form C. 2118

Place	Date	Hour	Summary of Events and Information	Remarks and references to Appendices
Hebuterne	1-27		General Routine Division at Rest.	
Hebuterne	28-31		"	

//DC 13

SECRET

Army Form C. 2118

WAR DIARY
or
INTELLIGENCE SUMMARY
(Erase heading not required.)

June 1916 Vol. N.115

Capt. A. A.D.S.S. 50th Division

WAR DIARY or INTELLIGENCE SUMMARY

Army Form C. 2118

Place	Date	Hour	Summary of Events and Information	Remarks and references to Appendices
Westoutre	June 1			
	2			
	3		Arranged with O.C. Salvage Co. for me to inspect all stores salvaged by him, so that serviceable stores may be re-issued to units requiring.	
	4			
	5			
	6			
	7		DDOS Second Army 92/42. All long rifles to be exchanged for short. Units asked number required.	
	8		Blankets now being returned to Base. 25% being retained by units.	
	9		Visited Salvage Co. and directed certain serviceable stores to be returned to me for re-issue.	
	10		Visited 4th Yorks + 4th Bn 2nd Yorks + instructed Quartermasters to return tent which were surplus. 2 from 4th Yorks + 1 from 4th Bn 2nd Yorks.	
	11		Visited 6th D.L.I. 8th D.L.I. (ordered 3 tents to be returned as only 3 & 5 men being used for each tent in possession) 7th Notts Fuseleers & 7th D.L.I. Surplus stores to be returned.	
	12			
	13			
	14		R. & K. wire forwarded showing 6028 short rifles & 6671 bayonets required to complete Infantry. Long rifles to be returned to Base.	

WAR DIARY
or
INTELLIGENCE SUMMARY

Army Form C. 2118

Place	Date	Hour	Summary of Events and Information	Remarks and references to Appendices
Westoutre	15		⎫ General Routine	
	16		⎬	
	17		⎭	
	18		Visited D.A.C.	
	19		" 4th Yorks	
	20		" Nobraye C.	
	21		" 6th N.F.	
	22		" 150th Brigade	
	23		" 151 "	
	24		" 149 "	
	25		⎫ General Routine	
	26		⎬	
	27		⎭	
	28			
	29			
	30			

A.D.M.S. 50th

Army Form C. 2118

WAR DIARY
or
INTELLIGENCE SUMMARY
(Erase heading not required.)

Capt. A. Ross ADW
P.A.D.O.S.
50th Division
July 1916. Volume 16

Vol 14

WAR DIARY or INTELLIGENCE SUMMARY

Army Form C. 2118

Place: Wetterlie

Date July	Hour	Summary of Events and Information	Remarks and references to Appendices
1		Visited Railway Co. 149 and 150 Bde Headquarters. Indented for 2 more Lewis guns for Ration Auth. O.B.9898 DOS making beach per Rath.	
2		Visited B Battery 252 Bde. All covered with exception of Rangefinder Artillery which had not yet been issued from programme. Wired.	
3		Indented for FH.G & one FH.G Helmets Auth. WMG QOS 31/26/A 30/6/16 to complete one per Officer and man, making one FH & one FH.G in possession of each Officer and man, excepting those having Box Respirators, who have a FH only.	
4		Visited 7th N'humberland Fusiliers and arranged for their armourer to report to me when necessary to repair rifles returned to me, there being no armourer's shop attached to the division.	
5		Instructed 6 Field Amb'ces required for a raid by 151 Bde.	
6		Visited 1, 2 + 3rd Field Ambulances.	

General Rankine

Army Form C. 2118

WAR DIARY
or
INTELLIGENCE SUMMARY
(Erase heading not required.)

Place	Date	Hour	Summary of Events and Information	Remarks and references to Appendices
Alexandria	July 13		} General Routine	
	14			
	15			
	16			
	17			
	18			
	19			
	20			
	21			
	22			
	23		Visited M.T. Vet. Sec.	
	24		Visited 150 Machine Gun Co. to try & determine Gun Co. to finally an amount of stores	
	25		& has been decided that no indents are to be accepted without the O.C. of each unit	
	26		signing for the demand. This has considerably reduced the demand for stores.	
	27		} General Routine	
	28			
	29			
	30			
	31			

WAR DIARY
or
INTELLIGENCE SUMMARY

(Erase heading not required.)

Army Form C. 2118

D.A.D.O.S
50th Division
August 1916

Vol 15
Vr No. 17

WAR DIARY
or
INTELLIGENCE SUMMARY
(Erase heading not required.)

Army Form C. 2118

Place	Date	Hour	Summary of Events and Information	Remarks and references to Appendices
Flexue	1-2		General Runtine	
	3		6 Vickers guns received to replace 6 Maxims. This completes all M.G. Co with Vickers guns 48 in all	
	4-5			
	6			
	7		Preparing to move to new area	
	8			
	9-17		Rondes shops at Caestre station for despatch to IX Corps Railhead. During this period moved to Bremenville, Vignacourt + Morlancourt (Somme)	
Morlancourt	18		Advises all units to submit in desk to complete establishment for all items including Wagon parts, technical artillery items etc in order to allow sufficient time for Base to send before division goes into action.	
	19		26 Lewis guns received completing each Battalion to 8 guns.	
	20-31		Division in training. General Runtine	

[Signature] Capt
ADVS
50/A

Vol 16

War Diary
or
Intelligence Summary

Capt. A.A. Roth
D.A.D.O.S
50th Div

September 1916

Army Form C. 2118

WAR DIARY
or
INTELLIGENCE SUMMARY
(Erase heading not required.)

Place	Date Sept.	Hour	Summary of Events and Information	Remarks and references to Appendices
Montigny	1		Division being issued with Steel Helmets asked army to supply being short. 200 asked in 3 days	
	2		A Bty 251 demands limn, Carriage sheet fittings to replace one destroyed through premature in bore	
	3		Lewis gun demanded by 4th Yorks to replace one condemned by armourer	
	4		All guns, machine guns now demanded in code and quickly issued to Base.	
	5		Lewis gun + 18pdr gun and carriage received 6 day demanded on the 2nd inst.	
	6		Finished 400 pairs of handles for rane to shellebs for ammunition from ground sheet may be improvised	
	7		Visited all Brigade Shops. all correct.	
	8		One 18pdr gun demanded to replace one condemned by 90A through casting for A 251 Bde.	
	9		Purchased 400 Knoßkanen for handles for 147 Pdr at 90 centimes each (Rent)	
	10		Purchased 6 large motoryneed straps for Divisional 14hp cars to Aeroplanes	
Mon M Clement	11		Moved to Sheet 62 D. 6.6.13. under Canvas.	
			Decided by Corps that all Running Oil Springs to keep D.A.D.O.S. dump + issue to 90A when required	
			by him for regunning guns	
	12		Finished 350 more Knotkaisen at 90 centimes each for 151 + 150 Brigades.	
	13		72 handcarts arrived making 144 completely established for heavier guns	
	14		One 18pdr gun demanded for A/251 condemned through wear and searing	

Army Form C. 2118

WAR DIARY
or
INTELLIGENCE SUMMARY
(Erase heading not required.)

Instructions regarding War Diaries and Intelligence Summaries are contained in F.S. Regs., Part II. and the Staff Manual respectively. Title Pages will be prepared in manuscript.

Place	Date	Hour	Summary of Events and Information	Remarks and references to Appendices
Hem.Millencourt Somme	15		3 Vickers demanded to replace destroyed by shell fire 150 Bde	
	16		2 " " " " " " " 149 "	
			2 Vickers 3" for 150 Bde and 2 Vickers 3" for 149 Bde demanded to replace destroyed by shell fire	
			5 Lewis guns to replace destroyed by shell fire for 6th Northd Fus. demanded	
			One 18 pdr gun with R.M. & with Carriage demanded to replace one condemned for premature wear	
			2 Lewis guns for 7th Northd Fus. demanded to replace destroyed by shell fire	
	17		1 3" Stokes for 149 Bde demanded to replace destroyed by shell fire	
			one Lewis gun for 4th East Yorks 3 for 5th Yorks 3 for 4th Yorks demanded to replace destroyed by shell fire	
			One 15 pdr gun Carriage for 13/251 demanded to replace one condemned by 20.III and to bare for extensive repair	
	19		6 Lewis guns for 9th DLI 2 for 5th Borders demanded to replace destroyed shell fire	
			1 Stokes 3" for 150 Bde demanded to replace destroyed shell fire	
			1 Lewis gun 9th DLI 9 over for 8th DLI demanded to replace destroyed shell fire	
	20		1 Lewis gun for 4th Yorks demanded to replace destroyed shell fire	
			The majority of these arrived within 24 hours. Gun was specially sent to Abbeville to collect those authorised by Havre to be issued by C.O. Abbeville.	

WAR DIARY
or
INTELLIGENCE SUMMARY
(Erase heading not required.)

Army Form C. 2118

Place	Date	Hour	Summary of Events and Information	Remarks and references to Appendices
New Millencourt	21		Owing to the large number of Lewis guns, Vickers & Hotchkiss becoming either unserviceable or destroyed by shell fire it would appear to be advisable to have a Corps reserve so that losses could be made at once and await 2 to 3 days before they could be replaced from the Base. One battalion lost as many as 6 out of the 8 Lewis guns.	
	22		2 Vickers 3" demounted to replace destroyed by 151 Bde	
	23		Vickers gun with carriage without B.M. for B 252 Bde condemned for wear & tearing	
	25		2 Lewis guns for 8th D.L.I demounted to replace destroyed by shell fire	
	26		1 - - 4th East Yorks -	
	27		5 Enemy Machine Guns captured by the division returned to base	
	28		5 Enemy Vickers Captured " " " "	
	29		9000 S.A.A. rounds received for infantry in front line trenches	
	30		78 sets of packsaddlery demanded for infantry on account of bad roads in area	

Vol 1917

CONFIDENTIAL

War Diary.
    D.A.D.O.S.
        50th Division

From   1st October 1916.
"   31st October 1916

Volume.   ~~XXX~~ ~~XXXI~~ ~~XIX~~

Army Form C. 2118

WAR DIARY
or
INTELLIGENCE SUMMARY
(Erase heading not required.)

Instructions regarding War Diaries and Intelligence Summaries are contained in F. S. Regs., Part II. and the Staff Manual respectively. Title Pages will be prepared in manuscript.

Place	Date	Hour	Summary of Events and Information	Remarks and references to Appendices
Mean Millencourt Unedi Canvas	1 2 3 4 5 6 7 8 9 10 11 12 13 14 15 16 17 18 19 20		General Routine	

1875 Wt. W593/826 1,000,000 4/15 J.B.C. & A. A.D.S.S./Forms/C. 2118.

Army Form C. 2118

WAR DIARY
or
INTELLIGENCE SUMMARY
(Erase heading not required.)

Instructions regarding War Diaries and Intelligence Summaries are contained in F. S. Regs., Part II. and the Staff Manual respectively. Title Pages will be prepared in manuscript.

Place	Date	Hour	Summary of Events and Information	Remarks and references to Appendices
Near Millencourt	21		⎫	
	22		⎬ General Routine	
	23		⎪	
	24		⎭	
Near Fricourt	25			
Mortar Camera	26			
	27		9th Divisional Artillery & the 1 Co. Tweem attached to me for administration	
	28		⎫	
	29		⎬ General Routine	
	30		⎪	
	31		⎭	

[signature] Capt
DADOS
5D

1875 Wt. W593/826 1,000,000 4/15 J.B.C. & A. A.D.S.S./Forms/C. 2118.

WAR DIARY
or
INTELLIGENCE SUMMARY
(Erase heading not required.)

Army Form C. 2118

Vol 18

Vol No 20

Capt A. A. ROTH
D.A.D.O.S. 50th Division

November 1916

WAR DIARY
or
INTELLIGENCE SUMMARY

Army Form C. 2118

Place	Date	Hour	Summary of Events and Information	Remarks and references to Appendices
Near Fricourt Mendscanon	1		Bradhead, Albert	
	2		Wired 9th DADOS to arrange all indents with clothing forward to 9th Artillery attached to one formation, situation	
	3			
	4			
	5		Genard Routine	
	6			
	7			
	8			
9 - 27				
	28		9th Artillery indents transferred to DADOS 50th Div being now administered by him	
	29		Genard Routine	
	30			

M Hert Capt
DADOS
50 x D

Army Form C. 2118

WAR DIARY
or
INTELLIGENCE SUMMARY
(Erase heading not required.)

Vol 19

Capt A. A. ROTH
DADOS 52nd Div
DECEMBER 1916

Vol 19 21

Place	Date	Hour	Summary of Events and Information	Remarks and references to Appendices

WAR DIARY or INTELLIGENCE SUMMARY

Army Form C. 2118

Place	Date	Hour	Summary of Events and Information	Remarks and references to Appendices
Banjeux Summer	1		Moved to Banjeux Division at Rest. Arranged with DADOS 15th Division to exchange Smoke Helmets	5000
	2		Tentage etc. in order to save transport during relief. Demanded 24 hour gives to complete division to 10 per battalion except 7th D.L.I. (Pioneer)	
	3		Authority DDOS 4th Army HD 30/3/2/13 29/1/16. As difficulties were experienced in replenishing tips running out arranged by DAC to the 9.O.M. I arranged that these were kept by me instead of the DAC and 9.O.M. demanded direct from me as required. My stock being kept up by demands from base. In this way every 15pdr gun becoming slightly unserviceable would be sent to the 9.O.M. and the fault generally was found not to be for the want of a spring. The formation of an Officers Clothing Depot at Fourth Army Headquarters has greatly relieved the demands for Officers Kits etc through this office and lessened correspondence through incorrect cargo arriving from base. General Rawlinson	
	5–12			
	13		Arranged with 9.O.M. III Corps to inspect all Field Kitchens in this division	
	14		As each Brigade packed all their Field Kitchens together, the 9.O.M. was able to inspect all in one day.	

WAR DIARY
or
INTELLIGENCE SUMMARY

(Erase heading not required.)

Army Form C. 2118

Place	Date	Hour	Summary of Events and Information	Remarks and references to Appendices
Bayeux	15		8 Field Kitchens were found to be unserviceable, & being sent to O.M's workshop for repair. One condemned and a new one demanded from the base.	
	15		D.R.O. in order to cancel all indents submitted prior to October 1st. Items still required to be re-demanded. Base advised.	
	16		Purchased canvas for making Carriers for Pack saddle to carry Rifles and # 5 ammunition to gun pits as indents were too bad for Vehicles. Arrangement made with Infantry Brigade to collect stores by G.S. wagon for the whole Brigade. Object: save transport, save coal and draw up separately, lighten work in store. General Grantline	
	17-24 25-30		A considerable saving in issue I understanding has been possible by only issuing Veh Parts, Chints and rocks in exchange for duty or unserviceable ones. The former being washed and re-issued, the latter returned to base.	
	31		Moved to 24 Rue Paul Knyelle Albert	

[signature] Capt D.A.D.O.S.

Vol 20

WAR DIARY

D.A.D.O.S. 50th Division

From 1 - 31st January 1917.

Volume XXII

Army Form C. 2118.

WAR DIARY
or
INTELLIGENCE SUMMARY.
(Erase heading not required.)

Capt. A. A. Roth A.S.D
DADOS 50th Div
January 1917

Vol 22

Army Form C. 2118

Vol 22. July

WAR DIARY
or
INTELLIGENCE SUMMARY
(Erase heading not required.)

Instructions regarding War Diaries and Intelligence Summaries are contained in F.S. Regs., Part II. and the Staff Manual respectively. Title Pages will be prepared in manuscript.

Place	Date	Hour	Summary of Events and Information	Remarks and references to Appendices
Allen Somme	1		Arrangements made to form Armourers shop. All armourers with exception of one to each Brigade to report to me for duty.	
	2		24 Lewis guns received to complete battalions to 12, except Pioneers.	
	3		Called for certificate from all units that vehicles are either in a serviceable condition or at the I.O.M. being repaired.	
	4		Arranged with O.C. Bath at Bergentin to send him 2000 sets of clean underclothing to be exchanged for dirty as men arrive for a bath.	
	5		Visited Qmaster stores and found a quantity of items being held in reserve and which were not required. These were ordered to be returned to mas is	
	6		850 Blankets 3 enemy rifles Greatcoats, clothing etc.	
	7			
	8			
	9		Owing to the laundry breaking down sufficient clean socks not being forthcoming I arranged with O.C. Baths to wash those at Bergentin Baths	
	10		48th Division Artillery attached to me for Ordce services, including DAC Mo'ly Tram & Field Ambulances 3 Field Coys and are heavier Battalion one lorry a W.O. & 2 men attached to me for the purpose	

Army Form C. 2118.

WAR DIARY
or
INTELLIGENCE SUMMARY.
(Erase heading not required.)

Instructions regarding War Diaries and Intelligence Summaries are contained in F. S. Regs., Part II. and the Staff Manual respectively. Title pages will be prepared in manuscript.

Place	Date	Hour	Summary of Events and Information	Remarks and references to Appendices
Albert (Aveluy)	11, 12		A fortnightly return showing number of boots required by each unit called for in order to compare demands & avoid excessive issues.	
	13		19th Labour Battalion attached to me for Ordnance services.	
	14		Arranged to hold the 149, 150 & 151 Reinforcement & training camps as three different units for Ordnance supplies in order to relieve the Infantry Brigade & respective units.	
	15		Demanded one 18 pounder complete with carriage for A/251 Bde to replace one destroyed by shell fire	
	16		Demanded one Vickers gun for 149 M.G.C. to replace one destroyed by shell fire	
	17		Demanded one Lewis gun for 5th Border to replace one destroyed by shell fire	
	18		Demanded one 18pdr gun for A/240 to replace one destroyed by shell fire (48th Divn)	
	19		" " " A/241 " " " " " " (")	
	20		" " " A/240 — condemned by DOM III Corps (")	
	21		" " " A/252 to replace one destroyed by shell fire (Afterwards cancelled)	
	22		Information received at conference with AOOS III Corps that division would move to a new area, and	demolition consequently
	23		that all Corps & area stores would be taken with by division owing to area being in Frenchfied	afterwards cancelled
	24		Arranged to transfer the whole of the Corps & area stores, Qr master stores, private kits, RE stores	
	25		including Tents, Anvers Mess, Gumboots Thigh to new area. 39 N.C.O's & men being granted me during this period, to cope with extra stores.	

A5834 Wt.W4973/M687 750,000 8/16 D. D. & L. Ltd. Forms/C.2118/13.

Army Form C. 2118.

WAR DIARY
or
INTELLIGENCE SUMMARY.
(Erase heading not required.)

Place	Date	Hour	Summary of Events and Information	Remarks and references to Appendices
Albert	26		Visited new area Fricourt & arranged to take over from French divisional DADVS	
Corrine	27		Owing to reorganization of Artillery D/252 became extinct A/252 became C/142 (48th Div) and B/252 became C/172 Bty (15th Div)	
	28		Owing to move to French area, stores suspended from Base	
	29		No bulk mines ready to leave army to move	
	30		All over and own stores loaded at G.H.Q. (new albert) 26 trucks in all	
	31		Visited new area, arranged billeting of Corps when staff	

Army Form C. 2118.

WAR DIARY
or
INTELLIGENCE SUMMARY.
(Erase heading not required.)

Vol 21
Vol XXIII
AOD.

Capt A. A. Roth.
DADOS 50th Div.

February 1917

WAR DIARY
or
INTELLIGENCE SUMMARY.

Army Form C. 2118.

Place	Date	Hour	Summary of Events and Information	Remarks and references to Appendices
Allal Feb Ribemont	1		Moved to Ribemont	
	2		Joined stores by lorry dried to units, in dump being available.	
	3		One Lewis gun demanded for 11th Batt Yorks to replace one condemned by armourer	
	4		Issue of clothes suspended owing to division moving to new area	
	5		24 Lewis guns demanded to complete all Infantry battalions to 14 guns per battalion excepting pioneers	
	6		Base wired to proceed with issue of stores	
	7		450 Lbs Iron nails were demanded for use in new area; received.	
	8		All cups and eyes and French signs required for new area demanded from base	
	9		1) Mountain Hunt/Vermorel (sprayers) 2) Ayres (Mrs.) (carpenters for ammunition dumps)	
	10		3) Rifle Grenade Clamps 4) Rifle Batteries 5) Blankets for Mg-mts 6) Fire Extinguishers	
	11		4) Linesmen 5) Farriers	
	12		5) Charges	
	13		Small Box respirators demanded to complete to one per officer and man	
TROYART	14		Moved to TROYART. Billed at La Flaque	
	15		100 Body Shields and 100 Helmets (Wolseley trough) received	
	16		24 Lewis guns received. This completes to 14 per battalion	

Army Form C. 2118.

WAR DIARY
or
INTELLIGENCE SUMMARY.

(Erase heading not required.)

Instructions regarding War Diaries and Intelligence Summaries are contained in F. S. Regs., Part II. and the Staff Manual respectively. Title pages will be prepared in manuscript.

Place	Date	Hour	Summary of Events and Information	Remarks and references to Appendices
TROVART	17		Owing to Thaw precautions Wagons & G.S. were used to draw stores from Rawlins	
	18		Finished 24 Buckets for use in front line, trailing walks out of trenches	
	19		1000 Small Box respirators received. HQrs asked for priority of issue to units as all respirators to complete division were not expected	
			to arrive at one time	
	20		Arranged for Ammunition shop to be attached close to my dump	
	21		One Armourer reporting to me from each Brigade	
	22-8		General Routine	

[signature] Capt.

Army Form C. 2118.

WAR DIARY
or
INTELLIGENCE SUMMARY.
(Erase heading not required.)

Vol 22

Captain A. A. ROTH. A.O.D.

DADOS

50th Division

March 1917

Army Form C. 2118.

WAR DIARY
or
INTELLIGENCE SUMMARY.
(Erase heading not required.)

Instructions regarding War Diaries and Intelligence Summaries are contained in F. S. Regs., Part II. and the Staff Manual respectively. Title pages will be prepared in manuscript.

Place	Date	Hour	Summary of Events and Information	Remarks and references to Appendices
PROYART	1		One Lewis gun each for 4th East Yorks and 5th Yorks received replacing others destroyed by shell fire	
	3		One 3" Stokes received for 149 Bde to replace one destroyed by shell fire	
	4		One Vickers gun received for 150 M.G. Coy – " – " –	
Meriancourt sur Somme	9		Rest area	
	12		24 Lewis guns received completing battalions to 16 guns each	
	13		Lewis gun handcarts returned to base and extra hundred B.O.Ways demanded in exchange	
	14		One Vickers gun received to replace one condemned by Armourer	
	15		B.O.C. orders all Stores Coys less 15% (for sick horses) to be returned to Ordnance	
	16		One enemy machine gun received for training purposes issued to 50th Nebatt.	
	17		All indents prior to those dated 1/1/17 cancelled have quick informed	
	25		All Cpn. Maskalest not required by units received and returned to III Corps Troops DRO 1808	
	26		All leather jerkins a second blankets ordered on pending move to III Army	
			4 trucks reported from RTD to convey Oldee stores constricting to new area.	

Army Form C. 2118.

WAR DIARY
or
INTELLIGENCE SUMMARY.
(Erase heading not required.)

Instructions regarding War Diaries and Intelligence Summaries are contained in F. S. Regs., Part II. and the Staff Manual respectively. Title pages will be prepared in manuscript.

Place	Date	Hour	Summary of Events and Information	Remarks and references to Appendices
Maricourt Sur Somme	27		Arranged to leave record blanket & heathy Jerkins with Town Major until required. 50th Arty Clery DAC 2.9.9.45 Mortar Btys, No1 Coy Train transferred to 56th Divn	
	28		All in dets transferred to DADOS 56th	
	29		Notification received that Third Army will be administered by Fourth Army from 31st	
	30		forwarded diver advanced parties to Millencourt Bois on way to new area	
	31		Moves to Millencourt Bois	

Army Form C. 2118.

WAR DIARY
or
INTELLIGENCE SUMMARY.
(Erase heading not required.)

Vol 23
Vol 25

Capt. A A ROTH AOD
DADOS 50th Division

April 1917

Army Form C. 2118.

WAR DIARY
or
INTELLIGENCE SUMMARY.
(Erase heading not required.)

Vol 25

Instructions regarding War Diaries and Intelligence Summaries are contained in F. S. Regs., Part II. and the Staff Manual respectively. Title pages will be prepared in manuscript.

Place	Date	Hour	Summary of Events and Information	Remarks and references to Appendices
April Mollien en Bois	1		Railhead Fachencourt.	
	2		Moved to Beauval	
	3		— Dompierre Railhead Fienvel	
	4		— Givenchy le Noble "	
Givenchy le Noble	5		All closes arrived during move by lorry to each Brigade from where units drew.	
	6		Administered by XVIII Corps Third Army.	
	7-11		Very few demands from units during move.	
Arras	12		Administered by VII Corps III Army. Railhead Noyer en Artois	
	15		14th Div Artillery transferred for Ordnance Services to 50th Div	
			48th A.F.A. Bde "	
			232 A.F.A. Bde "	
			7th Labour Coy (R.W.Surrey Regt)"	
			181 Tunnelling Coy "	

Army Form C. 2118.

WAR DIARY
or
INTELLIGENCE SUMMARY.
(Erase heading not required.)

Instructions regarding War Diaries and Intelligence Summaries are contained in F. S. Regs., Part II. and the Staff Manual respectively. Title pages will be prepared in manuscript.

Place	Date	Hour	Summary of Events and Information	Remarks and references to Appendices
April 15 Arras	15th		288 Army Troops Coy RE admitted to Ordnance Services by OAD05 50/12	
			25th Sanitary Section "	
			C Squad 19th Corps Cavalry "	
	16th		4 Vickers guns destroyed by shell fire of 1/51 Machine Gun Coy & demanded	
			10 Lewis guns destroyed & lost of 6 & D.L.I. and demanded	
	18th		5 Lewis guns destroyed of 6th N'thd Fusiliers and demanded	
			4 Vickers guns issued to 1/51 Machine Gun Coy and demanded	
			1 Vickers gun destroyed of 149 Machine Gun Coy	
	19th		288 Army Troops Coy RE transferred from 50th Divn to 56th Divn	
			232 A.F.A. Bde. transferred to 15th Division	
	20		5 Lewis guns issued to replace those lost on 18th to 6th N Fus	
			" " " " 16th to 6th D.L.I.	
			10 Lewis guns " " "	
	21		Russian bath issued to 149 Bde and 151 Bde for bathing men.	
	22.		Completion of return of all Blankets stored at Mericourt sur Somme.	
			One 4.5" How and carriage destroyed of D/146 Bde RFA and demanded.	

Army Form C. 2118.

WAR DIARY
or
INTELLIGENCE SUMMARY.
(Erase heading not required.)

Instructions regarding War Diaries and Intelligence Summaries are contained in F. S. Regs., Part II. and the Staff Manual respectively. Title pages will be prepared in manuscript.

Place	Date	Hour	Summary of Events and Information	Remarks and references to Appendices
Arras	23		One 4'5' How damaged by Shell fire of 10250 Bde RFA & remounted	
	24		Two 4'5' How damaged by shell fire of D250 Bde RFA & remounted	
			Two 18 pdrs damaged by shell fire of C 142 Bde RFA & remounted	
			Four Vickers guns destroyed by shell fire of 150 In. Bay & remounted	
			Two Vickers guns destroyed by shell fire of 149 In Bay & remounted	
			One Lewis gun destroyed by shell fire of 4th Yorks & remounted	
	25		One Div Artillery transferred from 50th Div to 14th for Ordnance Service	
			14th Div Army F.A. Bde — do —	
			450th Army F.A. Bde — do —	
			7th Lothian Bry. (R.W.S.R.) — do —	
			181 Tunnelling Coy — do —	
			25th Sanitary Section — do —	
			C Squad 19th Corps Cavalry — do —	
			One Lewis gun issued to 4th Yorks to replace one lost on 22nd August	
	26		Administered by XVIII Corps III Army Reckless Troop en Artois	
			Two Vickers guns issued to 149 In Bay to replace to lost on 24th	
			Four Vickers guns issued to 150 — do — do —	

Army Form C. 2118.

WAR DIARY
or
INTELLIGENCE SUMMARY.
(Erase heading not required.)

Instructions regarding War Diaries and Intelligence Summaries are contained in F. S. Regs., Part II. and the Staff Manual respectively. Title pages will be prepared in manuscript.

Place	Date	Hour	Summary of Events and Information	Remarks and references to Appendices
Doullens	27		Move of Ordnance Stores from Arras to Doullens	
	28		36 Lewis guns issued to 160 I. Bde to mercier unable to replace others lost on 25th	
	29		All Bdes visited and hastiered submittance of undents to complete establishment	

Vol 24

Vol 26

C.O.R.A. A. Roth ADD
7 ADDS 50th Division

May 1917

WAR DIARY
or
INTELLIGENCE SUMMARY.
(Erase heading not required.)

Army Form C. 2118.

VOL. 26

Place	Date	Hour	Summary of Events and Information	Remarks and references to Appendices
Contrelle	May 1st		2 Lewis guns issued to 8th O.B.L.I. to replace others lost in action	
Basseux	2		Move from Contrelle to Basseux. Administered by VII Corps	
"	3		Move from Basseux to Contrelle. Administered by XVIII Corps.	
Contrelle	4		The following was suggested to III Army on experiences gained.	

Thro DDOS III Army — Thro DDOS XVIII Corps.

In view of the shortage of Lewis Gun parts and continual losses of these in action, I visited all Battalions in this Division and interviewed their Lewis Gun Officers, Armourers and Adjutants.

I put it to them that all the parts in the spare part bag were not required in action and that only items enumerated in the attached list would likely to be required during actual operations. All without exceptions concurred.

(b) Re-issue this "First Aid Set" in lieu of complete spare part bags on request of

Place	Date	Hour	Summary of Events and Information	Remarks and references to Appendices
Ordnance	April		Letter to DDOS III Army	

A few of each of the other items are kept at my Armourers shops to attend to any guns that may require difficult repairs.

In view of the fact that Lewis Guns have to be hastily trained to replace casualties they could not be capable of repairing a gun unless very slightly out of order, which is allowed for in the "First Aid Set."

I beg therefore to submit that it would be more economical to issue to units a First Aid Set in lieu of a complete spare part bag, is kept of the other items being kept at Divisional Armourers Shop for more difficult repairs.

"Contents of a First Aid Set"
Spring Head screw & tangent sight
Pawl Feed arm
Pawl Spring
Front stop, magazine
return

Bolt, assembled
Casing piston
Spring Guide Cartridge

Army Form C. 2118.

WAR DIARY
or
INTELLIGENCE SUMMARY.
(Erase heading not required.)

Instructions regarding War Diaries and Intelligence Summaries are contained in F. S. Regs., Part II. and the Staff Manual respectively. Title pages will be prepared in manuscript.

Place	Date	Hour	Summary of Events and Information	Remarks and references to Appendices
Contescelle	May 4		Contents of First Aid Set Cont'd. Brush, Wire, rod cleaning cylinder, Spanish No. 1 M.C. Handle loading magazine, Wallet case spare parts box Handle wood, Can Oil Spanner Mouthpiece barrel. Gauge wire breech. Balance spring M.C. Discharger double.	
Contescelle	23		One Lewis Gun issued from Armourers Shop to replace one u/s to 4th East Yorks	
"	24		Move from Contescelle to Brun Administered by VIII Corps	

Army Form C. 2118.

WAR DIARY
or
INTELLIGENCE SUMMARY.

(Erase heading not required.)

Vol 27 Vol 2

Capt A A ROTH
DADOS
50th Divn

June 1917

Instructions regarding War Diaries and Intelligence Summaries are contained in F. S. Regs., Part II. and the Staff Manual respectively. Title pages will be prepared in manuscript.

Place	Date	Hour	Summary of Events and Information	Remarks and references to Appendices

Army Form C. 2118.

WAR DIARY
or
INTELLIGENCE SUMMARY.

(Erase heading not required.)

VOL. 27

Instructions regarding War Diaries and Intelligence Summaries are contained in F. S. Regs., Part II. and the Staff Manual respectively. Title pages will be prepared in manuscript.

Place	Date	Hour	Summary of Events and Information	Remarks and references to Appendices
Douin	1.6.17		2./ Enemy Machine guns. received for Instructional purposes.	
do	12.6.17		do do	
do	17.6.17		Move from Douin to Boisleaux au Mont	
Boisleaux Au Mont	18.6.17		Administered by VII Corps, III Army. The following units transferred from 18th Division to 50th Division for Administration :- No.1 Coy. 50th Div. Train V X Y & Z. Batteries 50th Trench Mortars 50th Div Ammunition Column HQrs 250 Bde. R.F.A. A B C & D Batteries HQrs 251. Bde R.F.A. A B C & D Batteries No.1. Coy. 14th Div. Train V X Y & Z. Batteries 14th Trench Mortars	

WAR DIARY
or
INTELLIGENCE SUMMARY.
(Erase heading not required.)

Army Form C. 2118.

Place	Date	Hour	Summary of Events and Information	Remarks and references to Appendices
Bousleaux au Mont	18.6.17		Units transferred from 18th to 50th Division continued as under :- 14th Divisional Ammunition Column. H Qrs 46th Bde. R.F.A. ABC&D Batteries H Qrs 47th Bde. R.F.A. ABC&D Batteries 181. Tunnelling Coy R.E. D.R.O 1990. Re Rifle Covers. Every rifle must either have an all over cover or a breech cover. All units equipped with same.	
"	18.6.17			
"	24.6.17		D.R.O 2083. Vehicles, overhaul and repair of	
"	26.6.17		18 Pdr. Gun demanded for B/46. Bde. R.F.A to replace one destroyed by shell fire.	
"	"		Inspector of Armourers, Lieut Field A.O.D, visited Brigades and found all Machine guns, rifles etc in good condition	

Army Form C. 2118.

WAR DIARY
or
INTELLIGENCE SUMMARY.
(Erase heading not required.)

Place	Date	Hour	Summary of Events and Information	Remarks and references to Appendices
Boisleux au Mont	24.6.17		D.R.O 2087. Tentage return rendered thro' Q Office	
	28.6.17		One Lewis gun destroyed by shell fire of 5th D.L.I and demanded	Issue from Armourers Shop
			" " " " "	"
			" " " " " 5th Yorks	"
			" " " " " 5 Yorks and demanded	
	29th		One Vickers gun destroyed by shell fire of 150 M.G.Coy and demanded	
			Two Lewis guns " " 4th Yorks and demanded	
			HQrs 14th D.A.	
			A. B.C+D Batteries 46 Bde R.F.A	
			A.B.C+D " 49 Bde R.F.A	
			HQrs 14 D.A.C & All Sections } Transferred to IX Corps.	
			No 1 Coy 14th Divl Train	
			X Y + Z Batteries 14th Trench Mortars	

WAR DIARY
or
INTELLIGENCE SUMMARY

Army Form C. 2118.

Vol 26

Vol 28

Capt. A A ROTH
D A D O S
50th
July 1917

WAR DIARY
or
INTELLIGENCE SUMMARY.
(Erase heading not required.)

Army Form C. 2118.

Place	Date	Hour	Summary of Events and Information	Remarks and references to Appendices
Boisleux au Mont	2/7/17		3 Lewis Guns demanded for 4th East Yorks Regt. and received to replace destroyed.	
			1 Vickers Gun demanded for 149 M. Gun Coy.	
	5/7/17		1 Lewis Gun demanded for 4 East Yorks Regt.	
	6/7/17		1 18 Pdr. demanded for C/251 Bde. for scoring.	
			1 3" Stokes Mortar demanded for 151 T.M. Battery to replace one destroyed.	
	8/7/17		2 3" Stokes Mortars demanded for 150 T.M. Battery to replace condemned.	
			1 Lewis Gun received for 4 East Yorks Regt.	
	10/7/17		1 Vickers Gun received for 150 Machine Gun Coy.	
			Anti Gas Goggles (all patterns) obsolete and being withdrawn.	
	11/7/17		150 Infantry Bde. inspection of all arms by Brent. Field AOD	
	12/7/17		2 3" Stokes Mortars received for 150 #1 Gun Coy. T. Mortar Bty.	
	13/7/17		Brent. Field AOD inspected all arms 1st Div. Infy.	
			149 Brigade inspection of arms by Brent. Field AOD	
			Gt. Divisional Artillery (less T.M. Byds) moved to the Som Fm. administrative Hq 17 Division.	

WAR DIARY or INTELLIGENCE SUMMARY

Army Form C. 2118.

Place	Date	Hour	Summary of Events and Information	Remarks and references to Appendices
Brielen Au Mont	14/7		Visited Brigades and Battalions, nothing of importance outstanding	
	15/7		Lieut. Zell A.O.D. visited 6th and 7th North'd. Fus. and inspected at Aama.	
			1S Mts and Carriage demanded for C/51 Bde to replace destroyed by shell fire (whole PM)	
	17/7		Stokes Howitzer received for 151 T. Mortar Bty	
	18/7		Conference at Office of A.D.O.S.	
			1 Lewis Gun demanded for 4th Yorks Regt to replace destroyed shell fire	
	19/7		1 Lewis Gun demanded for 4th Yorks Regt "	
			2 Lewis Guns " 5th Yorks Regt "	
			2 Lewis Guns " 6th D.L.I. "	
	20/7		1 RFU demanded for A/250 Bde (without BM) (condemned) 1st Storag	
			1 " " B/251 " " "	
			1 " " B/251 " " "	
			6 Lewis Guns received for 4th Yorks, 5th Yorks and 6th D.L.I.	
	21/7		Sent Field A.O.D. visited 151 M.G. Coy and inspected Vickers Guns.	
	22/7		Field A.O.D. left for duty with 2nd Division.	
	23/7		1 Lewis Gun demanded for 4th North'd. Fus. to replace destroyed by shell fire	
			1 Stokes Howitz. received for 150 T.M. Battery.	

Army Form C. 2118.

WAR DIARY
or
INTELLIGENCE SUMMARY.
(Erase heading not required.)

Place	Date	Hour	Summary of Events and Information	Remarks and references to Appendices
Bivalent au Mont	24/7		1 Lewis Gun demanded for 4th North. Fus. to replace destroyed by hostile fire	
	26/7		2 Lewis Guns received for 4th North. Fus.	
	"		1 Vickers Gun demanded for 180 M. Gun Coy to replace destroyed by shell fire.	
	"		1 18 pdr without B.M. demanded for B/251 Bde. damaged by shell fire.	
	29/7		1 18 pdr without B.M. demanded for B/250 Bde. Condemned for scoring.	
	"		1 18 pdr Carriage for B/50 Bde demanded to replace damaged by hostile fire	

Army Form C. 2118.

WAR DIARY
or
INTELLIGENCE SUMMARY.
(Erase heading not required.)

Vol 27

Capn. A.A. Roth
DADOS
50th Divn

Vol 29

Lt. Col. Anthony

Army Form C. 2118.

WAR DIARY
or
INTELLIGENCE SUMMARY
(Erase heading not required.)

Volume 28

Place	Date	Hour	Summary of Events and Information	Remarks and references to Appendices
Bois Leau Cu Mont	August 2		Move from 50th Division to 7th 4th Corps of the 9th Ord Artilly for administration. HQrs ABC&D Batteries 501th R.F.A. 51 Bde R.F.A. A B C & D " " 9th DA Column HQrs 1st & 2nd DA Echelon 9th DA Column No 1 Coy 9th Divn Train	
	4/th		Move from VII Corps troops to 50th Division of the undermentioned units: 29th Reserve Park 58th, 21st and 41st Chinese Sub Parks, 20 Reserve R.E. 60th Sanitary Section. 'G' M.G. O.Boys. 3rd M.tn Ambulance Convoy 20th & 43rd Casualty Clearing Stns, 38th 45th and 70th Sanitary Sections 44th, 45th and 62nd Labour Groups, 11th, 18th, 80th, 115th, 119th, 126th, 188th and 190th Infantry Labour Coys, 14th and 18th Waza Labour Coys	
	5th		One 18 pmder O.F. Rem condemned by .SQM.F. E250 Be R.F.A and one demanded to replace	
	11/9		One 3" Stokes Mortar Condemned by SQM F. 150. I.M. Coy and one demanded to replace	

WAR DIARY or INTELLIGENCE SUMMARY

Army Form C. 2118.

Vol. 28.

Place	Date	Hour	Summary of Events and Information	Remarks and references to Appendices
Bresleau Ou Mont	15th Aug 1917		Move from 4th Division to 50th Division to HQrs 23rd Army F.A. Bde. 108 Battery 23rd Bde for administrative purposes. 2 Lew Pty " " One Vickers Gun (condemned by Armourer, and demanded of) 151 Machine Gun Coy.	
	21st "			
	23rd "		Move from 50th Division to XIV Corps Troops of 75th Infantry Labour Company. One Vickers Gun received to replace one condemned with 21st of 15th Machine Gun Coy.	
	25"		Move from 50th Division to XIV Corps Troops of 75th Sanitary Sanitary Section for administration. One 18 pounder and carriage demanded to replace one condemned by IOM for formation of A/251 Bde R.F.A.	

WAR DIARY
or
INTELLIGENCE SUMMARY.

Army Form C. 2118.

Place	Date	Hour	Summary of Events and Information	Remarks and references to Appendices
Ourlies Aumont	28		One L. 5" How: Carriage Condemned for Damage by M.T. ordered for D/250 Bde R.F.A. by G.O.M. and demanded for D/250 Bde R.F.A. One 18 pdr. Carriage Condemned for Damage by hostile fire by A.O.M. and demanded for A/250 Bde R.F.A.	

Army Form C. 2118.

WAR DIARY
or
INTELLIGENCE SUMMARY.

(Erase heading not required.)

Vol 28

Capt. A.A. ROTH.
DADOS 50th Div.

Vol 30

September 1917

Place	Date	Hour	Summary of Events and Information	Remarks and references to Appendices

WAR DIARY
or
INTELLIGENCE SUMMARY.

Army Form C. 2118.

(Erase heading not required.)

Summary of Events and Information Volume. 30

Place	Date	Hour	Summary of Events and Information	Remarks and references to Appendices
Acheux en Amiénois	2/7/17		The following DRO No 3216 was published on Officers Equipment on page 1. The following items are available at Army Clothing Stops Deulette and can be obtained on Indication of Form W.3225 duly signed. Where an officer is unable to call at the Stops personally the Representative can obtain any article by producing signed voucher A.B.F. 50 duly on form W.3225. These can be obtained from D.A.D.O.S. — Compass Prismatic £ 2.10.9 Binoculars £ 6. 5 "MK II" Special £ 2. 7. 6 Pistols Webley MK VI £ 2. 3. 5	
	9/7		Move from 50th Division to 10th Corps Troops for administration. 21st Army Sat Rock.	

WAR DIARY or INTELLIGENCE SUMMARY

Army Form C. 2118.

Place	Date	Hour	Summary of Events and Information	Remarks and references to Appendices
Reninghelst Huts	9/3/17		Move from 2nd Corps Troops to 50th Division of 2nd Special Coy R.E. for administration.	
"	10/3/17		Lieut Major Mercatel Bresleau Bel Mont taken on lot of unit for administration (while in VI Corps).	
"	16/3/17		Move from 3rd Division to 50th Division of the following units. C By 23 A.T.M.Bde and 107 By 23rd M Bde. D.R.O. No 3265 published re Returns (Reserves & Stores) &c. It is observed that demands are received from units for the replacement of technical stores, angle irons, etc. without the receipt being attached to the intended demand, that the units concerned in future take receipts must be attached when submitting demands, unless to do so would be to the satisfaction of the D.A.D.O.S that it is not desirable to return the articles before the receipt of the new, and in this case the upset items as soon after the receipt of the new as possible.	

Place	Date	Hour	Summary of Events and Information	Remarks and references to Appendices
Bioleau Au Mont	16/9		DRO 3265 Continued As regards Batt stores w/s items are to be delivered within two weeks after came of new for infantry M.G.lys and R.E. units and within one week for other units. One 18 pdr Gun Carriage demanded for C/250 Bde R.F.A. to replace condemned by LMW	
	17/9		One 4".5" hows received for D/250 Bde R.F.A.	
	18/9			
	20/9		C Bty 23 A.F.A. Bde. moved to 16th Division	
	22/9		Four 2" Trench Mortars demanded to replace condemned and destroyed for 249 50 Inf. Bde. 107 Bty A.F.A. Bde moved from 50th Divn to 62nd Division	
	26/9		One 18 pdr Gun demanded for A/251 Bde R.F.A. to replace condemned One two gun Carriage demanded for 6 Dt L. to replace destroyed 5" Bdus "	
	27/9		One 18 pdr gun Carriage demanded for B 251 Bde R.F.A. to replace / condemned by LMW.	

WAR DIARY
or
INTELLIGENCE SUMMARY.

Army Form C. 2118.

Place	Date	Hour	Summary of Events and Information	Remarks and references to Appendices
Bresleu Au Mont	27/9		One 4'5 How Carriage demanded to replace Condemned for 91/251 Bde. One Lewis gun received for 6th Dv. J. 3 Trench Mortars 2" received for 50 Inn Bde. L and K sections No 3 Special by R.E. transferred to III Corps troops. 20 Reserve Park transferred to III Corps troops.	

Army Form C. 2118.

WAR DIARY
or
INTELLIGENCE SUMMARY.
(Erase heading not required.)

Vol 29
Vol 31
Vol 30

Capt. A. A. Roth
A.D.M.S. 50th Division

October 1917

Army Form C. 2118.

WAR DIARY
or
INTELLIGENCE SUMMARY.
(Erase heading not required.)

Instructions regarding War Diaries and Intelligence Summaries are contained in F. S. Regs., Part II. and the Staff Manual respectively. Title pages will be prepared in manuscript.

Place	Date	Hour	Summary of Events and Information	Remarks and references to Appendices
Bordeaux Aumont	3rd 19__ 4th		18 pdr Gun demanded for 108 Bty 23 AFA Bde to replace one condemned. Move from III Corps Troops to 56th Division of J and M Sections No. 3 Special Coy R.E.	
	5th	18 pdr	Gun demanded for A.251 Bdr RFA to replace one condemned.	
	6th		Move from 50th to 51st Division for administration.— 3 Qrs. I.M. Section No 3 Special Coy R.E. 181 Grounding Coy R.E. No 1 23rd AFA Bde 108 Bty " " A Bty " " 23 AFA Bde Ammn Column Nos 1, 2 +3 Sections 27 Reserve Park 41st Ammn Sub Park 60th Aux Steam Coy ASC M.T. 3rd Motor Ambulance Convoy 20th Casualty Clearing Stns 43rd " "	

Army Form C. 2118.

WAR DIARY
or
INTELLIGENCE SUMMARY.
(Erase heading not required.)

Instructions regarding War Diaries and Intelligence Summaries are contained in F.S. Regs., Part II. and the Staff Manual respectively. Title pages will be prepared in manuscript.

Place	Date	Hour	Summary of Events and Information	Remarks and references to Appendices
Boeschepe Cas Mont	6/9/17		Units Moved from 50th Division to 51st Division continued:— 38th Sanitary Section 70th " " 45 Labour Group 62 " " 11th Infy Labour Coys 125 " " " 183 " " " 190 " " " 37th Noyon Labour Coys 35th " " " Gun 18 pdr demanded for B. 250 Bde R.F.A to replace condemned	
	7/9/17		Move completed of Ordnance Stores to Achiet le Petit	
	12/9/17		S.R.O 3378 1st Sept 1917 All entries for Ordnance Stores prior to should be redemanded in the usual manner. Any item still required	

Army Form C. 2118.

WAR DIARY
or
INTELLIGENCE SUMMARY.
(Erase heading not required.)

Instructions regarding War Diaries and Intelligence Summaries are contained in F. S. Regs., Part II. and the Staff Manual respectively. Title pages will be prepared in manuscript.

Place	Date	Hour	Summary of Events and Information	Remarks and references to Appendices
Achiet le Petit Edgehill	15/10/17		18 pdr Gun demanded for C/251 Bde to replace condemd.	
	16/10/17		Move of Ordnance Stores from Achiet le Petit to Edgehill	
	18/10/17		Six Gun Carriages received from Ordnance Gun Park	
			Army to complete outstanding indents of Divisions	
			18 pdr Guns received from Calais & Base to replace	
			old outstanding indents of Divisions	
			Administered by II Corps V Army	
			Winter Clothing demanded for the above divisions	
	20/10/17		Move of Ordnance Stores from Edgehill to Proven	
	22/10/17		18 pdr Sights & Carriage demanded for C/49 Bde R.F.A. to	
Proven			replace one totally destroyed by shell fire	
	23/10/17		ditto	
Elverdinghe	24/10/17		Move of Ordnance Stores from Proven to Elverdinghe	

WAR DIARY or INTELLIGENCE SUMMARY

Army Form C. 2118.

Place	Date	Hour	Summary of Events and Information	Remarks and references to Appendices
Elverdinghe	24/7/17		Administered by 14th Corps.	
	25/7/17		18 pdr gun & carriage demanded for A/76 Bde RFA to replace totally destroyed. 18 pdr Gun Carriage demanded for C/76 Bde RFA to replace totally destroyed. 18 pdr Gun Carriage demanded for B/79 Bde RFA to replace totally destroyed. 4.5" Howitzer & carriage demanded for B/79 Bde RFA to replace totally destroyed.	
	26/7/17		4.5" How. Carriage demanded for B/251 Bde RFA to replace totally destroyed by premature. Two Vickers Guns demanded for 149 MGCoy, and received.	
	27/7/17			
	28/7/17		Administered by 19th Corps.	

Place	Date	Hour	Summary of Events and Information	Remarks and references to Appendices
Clandeboye	28/9		Three Vickers Guns demanded to replace destroyed by shell fire.	
	29/9		Eleven Lewis Guns demanded for 4th A. from Co to replace destroyed by shell fire. Six Lewis Guns demanded for 5 D.L.I. to replace destroyed by shell fire.	

K.F. Plott
Capt.

Army Form C. 2118.

WAR DIARY
or
INTELLIGENCE SUMMARY.
(Erase heading not required.)

Vol 30

Cap A A Neth
DADOS 50 Division
November 1917.

Vol 32

Place	Date	Hour	Summary of Events and Information	Remarks and references to Appendices

Instructions regarding War Diaries and Intelligence Summaries are contained in F. S. Regs., Part II. and the Staff Manual respectively. Title pages will be prepared in manuscript.

Army Form C. 2118.

WAR DIARY
or
INTELLIGENCE SUMMARY.
(Erase heading not required.)

Place	Date	Hour	Summary of Events and Information	Remarks and references to Appendices
Blaringhem	1/7		One 18 pdr Gun demanded to replace one destroyed by shell fire for C/149 Bde R.F.A.	
"	3/7		do	
"	4/7		One 18 pdr Gun demanded for C/251 Bde to replace one destroyed by shell fire	
"	7/7		One 18 pdr Gun Carriage demanded for A/146 Bde R.F.A. to replace one damaged by storm	
"	9/7		Move from 50th Division to 19th Division of all 50th Artillery and 3rd Field Ambulance, 1 D.L.F. Field Coy R.E. and 4th E. Yorks.	
"	10/7		Move from Blaringhem to Eperlecques in exchequer of ordnance stores	
			Administered by XVIII Corps	
Eperlecques	11/7		Chaff Cutters to be issued to all units and retained	

A 5634 Mt.W4973/M687 750,000 8/16 D. D. & L. Ltd. Forms/C.2118'13.

Army Form C. 2118.

WAR DIARY
or
INTELLIGENCE SUMMARY.
(Erase heading not required.)

Instructions regarding War Diaries and Intelligence Summaries are contained in F. S. Regs., Part II. and the Staff Manual respectively. Title pages will be prepared in manuscript.

Place	Date	Hour	Summary of Events and Information	Remarks and references to Appendices
	17/7		Military Medals awarded to Cpl Gallacher N°M/103592 & Dvr Stevenson and Rt Allan #5923 6th DLI & Both attached to me for duty	
	18/7		Move from 19th Corps Troops to 50th Division for administration of 4th York & Lancs Pioneers	
	25/7		Move from 18th Corps Troops to 50th Division. 12th R.O.Y.L.I. Pioneers for administration & 4th and 446 Field Coys. R.E. from 50th	
			Move of H.Q. and 446 Field Coys R.E. to 17th Division	
	28/7		Move from 14th to 50th Division of 3rd Field Ambulance	
	30/7		Move of H.Q. and 446 Field Coys R.E. from 17th to 50th Division	

Army Form C. 2118.

WAR DIARY
or
INTELLIGENCE SUMMARY.
(Erase heading not required.)

Vol 31

Capt A A ROTH
DADOS
50th Division

Vol 33

December 1917

WAR DIARY
or
INTELLIGENCE SUMMARY.
(Erase heading not required.)

Army Form C. 2118.

Place	Date	Hour	Summary of Events and Information	Remarks and references to Appendices
Ecoivres	2/7/17		Area Commandants Ecoivres Administered by 50th Division	
"	3/7/17		Move from 50th Division to 31st Division of 12th Bn. 1st R.O. Yorkshire R. Ecoivres for administration	
"	4/7/17		Move from 11th Division to 56th Division of 7th D.L.I. and 3rd 1/4th Field Ambulance for administration	
"	5/7/17		Move from Corps Division to II Corps Troops of the following units of Artillery:—
VX/X/42 Batteries
50th L.M. Sec.
H.Q.s 50th D.A.
250 Bde RFA
251 do do
H.Q.s & 1/3, 1, 2 & SAH Sections No1 Coy ASC Dvl Trains
50 D.A. Columns	

Army Form C. 2118.

WAR DIARY
or
INTELLIGENCE SUMMARY.
(Erase heading not required.)

Instructions regarding War Diaries and Intelligence Summaries are contained in F. S. Regs., Part II. and the Staff Manual respectively. Title pages will be prepared in manuscript.

Place	Date	Hour	Summary of Events and Information	Remarks and references to Appendices
Opalesque	6/7		Move from 19th Division to 35th Division for administration for all units of 50th D.A. including H.Q. of Division	
"	8/7		Move from 35th Division to 58th Division for administration of all units of the 50th D.A.	
"	9/7		Move from 50th Division to 19th Division for administration	
			Area for remainder:	
			Water	M/15 Bruce Farm
			Moille	H.Q. Gibson Ck.
			Byrus	" " Can Purchase Bris 356
			"	14th "
			Surnham	Det. No. 9 Area Stamboy & 780 Area Employment Co
			Mordasque	56th Sanitary Section & Army Bucksights
			Hautecques	V Army M Musketry Camp No. 1 Reinforced Rest Camp
				50th Depot Bn. Ca York & ancres Regt.
				65 Catron Group H.Q.
				1st Middlesex Lab. Coy.
				29th Prisoners of War Camp
				45 " "
				56 " "
			All the units were attached from 16 G.H.Q. on the first	

A5834 Wt. W4973/M687 750,000 8/16 D. D. & L. Ltd. Forms/C.2118/13.

WAR DIARY
or
INTELLIGENCE SUMMARY.
(Erase heading not required.)

Army Form C. 2118.

Place	Date	Hour	Summary of Events and Information	Remarks and references to Appendices
Eperlecque	13/7		Move from Eperlecque to Brandhoek of 50th Division	
Brandhoek	14/7		Administered by 8th Corps troops	
"	17/7		Move from 58th Division to 50th Division for administration	
			HQrs 50th DA	
			250 Bde RFA	
			251 " "	
			All Section DAC	
			V,X,Y + Z TM Batteries	
			1st by Divl Train	
"	4/7		Move from 33rd DA to 50th Division for administration	
			HQrs 33 DA	Norboy Q.86
			156 Bde RFA	V/12 field by RE
				212 " "
			X,Y + Z TM Batteries	222 " "
			162 " " DAC	Lbrs 33 RE
			All Section DAC	18th Middlesex Pioneers

Army Form C. 2118.

WAR DIARY
or
INTELLIGENCE SUMMARY.
(Erase heading not required.)

Place	Date	Hour	Summary of Events and Information	Remarks and references to Appendices
Bouzincourt	14/4 24/4/17		Move from 33rd Division to 50th Division. HQrs 39th DA All Sections DAC 174 Bde RFA No1 coy ASC mt. 156 " VXY+Z TM Batteries Move from 50th Division to 39 Division for administration. 180 Bde RFA 19th Bde RFA All Sections DAC VXYZ TM Batteries	
	24/4		Move from 50th Division to 35th Division for administration	

Capt VOS 50

Vol I 19

Confidential

War Diary

of

A.D. of V.S, 50th Division

from 1.1.17 to 31.1.17

Vol. ~~XVI~~

Army Form C. 2118.

WAR DIARY
or
INTELLIGENCE SUMMARY.
(Erase heading not required.)

WA 32

Volume 35

Captain AA Roth
DADOS 50 Division
January 1918.

Army Form C. 2118.

WAR DIARY
or
INTELLIGENCE SUMMARY.
(Erase heading not required.)

Volume No 35

Instructions regarding War Diaries and Intelligence Summaries are contained in F.S. Regs., Part II. and the Staff Manual respectively. Title pages will be prepared in manuscript.

Place	Date	Hour	Summary of Events and Information	Remarks and references to Appendices
BRANDHOEK	1st Jan 1918 to 18th Jan 1918		General Routine work	
WIZERNES	19th Jan 1918 to 29th Jan 1918		General Routine work	
BRANDHOEK	30/31st Jan 1918		General Routine work	
			Nothing of importance to report.	

ABrak Capt
ADOS 50 Division

WAR DIARY
or
INTELLIGENCE SUMMARY.
(Erase heading not required.)

Army Form C. 2118.

DADMS 50

Volume XXXV Vol 3

Capt A. A. Roth
DADMS 50th Division
February 19

Volume No. 35

Army Form C. 2118.

WAR DIARY
or
INTELLIGENCE SUMMARY.
(Erase heading not required.)

Instructions regarding War Diaries and Intelligence Summaries are contained in F. S. Regs., Part II. and the Staff Manual respectively. Title pages will be prepared in manuscript.

Place	Date	Hour	Summary of Events and Information	Remarks and references to Appendices
BRANDHOEK	1st Feb		General Routine Work	
	2"		" " "	
	3rd		" " "	
	4th		" " "	
	5th		" " "	
	6th		" " "	
	7th		" " "	
	8th		" " "	
	9th		Move of 9th Durham L.I. to 62nd Division	
	10"		" of 5th Border Regt to 66th Division	
	11"		" of 7th North Fus to 42nd Division	
	to		General Routine Work	
	19"			

WAR DIARY
or
INTELLIGENCE SUMMARY.

(Erase heading not required.)

Army Form C. 2118.

Place	Date	Hour	Summary of Events and Information	Remarks and references to Appendices
BRANDOEK	20/7/8		29 Lewis Guns issued to various administrative units, Infantry Bttns and R.F.A. Batterys.	
	23rd		Move from Brandoek to Wyepres	
	24th to 28th		General Routine work	

Army Form C. 2118.

WAR DIARY
or
INTELLIGENCE SUMMARY.
(Erase heading not required.)

Vol 36 Vol 34

C.R.A. War Diary
A.D.C.S. 50th Div
March 1918

/ **WAR DIARY**
or
INTELLIGENCE SUMMARY.
(Erase heading not required.)

Army Form C. 2118.

Volume 36

Place	Date	Hour	Summary of Events and Information	Remarks and references to Appendices
Wygnes	1/18 3/18		Administered by 8th Corps. The following DRO was published:— <u>INDENTS FOR ORDNANCE STORES</u> No. 3782. In order to effect economy it is imperative that everything possible should be done to keep down Ordnance demands. Indents for replacement of unserviceable stores should be carefully scrutinised by Commanding Officers and the orders inforce regarding the return of the damaged or worn out articles requiring to be replaced should be most strictly observed. The attention of all units is directed to <u>DRO 3265</u> The following procedure regarding demands for all detail items must in future be strictly observed. Demands to Replace unserviceable } Demands for replacement must be supported by receipt shewing that the unserviceable store has been returned otherwise indents cannot be accepted by DADOS	

Place	Date	Hour	Summary of Events and Information	Remarks and references to Appendices
Wiryins	3/8		DRO 3782 (Continued) Demands to Replace Losses	

Must be supported by a statement signed by OC unit concerned explaining circumstances under which the Losses occurred.

As regards tent stores, the number of unserviceable articles of service issue clothing, Boots etc. returned are much below the number of new articles issued.

Every endeavour must be made by units to return the same number of old articles as are demanded as replacement.

The procedure regarding Boot stores as detailed in DRO 3265 will continue until further notice.

WAR DIARY
or
INTELLIGENCE SUMMARY.
(Erase heading not required.)

Army Form C. 2118.

Place	Date	Hour	Summary of Events and Information	Remarks and references to Appendices
Woyennes	4/3/18		General Routine Work	
	6 3/18			
	8 3/18		Move from Woyennes to Montuel	
	9 3/18		Administered by OOJ.S. Army	
Montuel	10 3/18		Move from Montuel to Harbonnières	
Harbonnières	14 3/18		Centre administrative unit covered with Machine Guns	
"	19 3/18		50 AA Office	
			50th Divl Artillery administered by OO 19th Corps Troops.	
"	20 3/18		18 pdr Gun demanded for B.250 Bde RFA to replace one	
			destroyed by Shell fire	
"	21 3/18		Move from Harbonnières to Le Mesnil near Rouvres	
"	22 3/18		Move to Villers Carbonnel	
			Move from Villers Carbonnel to Chaulnes	
			Move from Chaulnes to Foucaucourt	
"	23 3/18		Move from Foucaucourt to Harbonnières	

WAR DIARY
or
INTELLIGENCE SUMMARY

Army Form C. 2118.

Place	Date	Hour	Summary of Events and Information	Remarks and references to Appendices
	24/3/18		Move from Matomino to Foucaucourt. Machine Guns issued direct from Gun Park to units	
	"		Move from Foucaucourt to Villers Bretonneux	
	25/3/18		Move from Villers Bretonneux to Blangy Tronville	
	26/3/18		Machine Guns drawn from Gun Park which was urgently required during heavy bombing raid by hostile aircraft and delivered to 50th M.G.Bn.	
	27/3/18		Move from Blangy Tronville to Villers Bretonneux. Machine Guns drawn from Gun Park and issued direct to units.	
	28/3/18		Move from Villers Bretonneux to Boves	
			Move from Boves to La Motty	
	29/3/18		Move from La Motty to Boves. Machine Guns drawn from Gun Park and issued direct to units	
	30/3/18		Move from Boves to Sains Amiens	
	31/3/18		Move from Sains Amiens to Doury for re-equipment of Divisions	

Army Form C. 2118.

WAR DIARY
or
INTELLIGENCE SUMMARY.
(Erase heading not required.)

Volume 31.
Capt. A. A. ROTH
A.A. PADOS
50th Division

April 1918.

Army Form C. 2118.

WAR DIARY
or
INTELLIGENCE SUMMARY.
(Erase heading not required.)

Instructions regarding War Diaries and Intelligence Summaries are contained in F. S. Regs., Part II. and the Staff Manual respectively. Title pages will be prepared in manuscript.

Place	Date	Hour	Summary of Events and Information	Remarks and references to Appendices
Doury	1/8		Marked progress made in re-equipment of Division all Lewis Vickers guns issued to complete units also Trench Mortars	
Robecq	5/8		Administered by XVIII Corps General Routine Work	
	to		Administered by 15th Corps	
Merville	8/8			
	9/8		Heavy Shell fire by enemy, move to Chateau outside Merville	
	12/8		Move from Chateau Merville to La Motte	
	13/8		Move from La Motte to Thiennes Vickers Guns issued to units direct	
	18/8		Move from Thiennes to Witte Administered by 15th Corps	

Army Form C. 2118.

WAR DIARY
or
INTELLIGENCE SUMMARY.
(Erase heading not required.)

Instructions regarding War Diaries and Intelligence Summaries are contained in F. S. Regs., Part II. and the Staff Manual respectively. Title pages will be prepared in manuscript.

Place	Date	Hour	Summary of Events and Information	Remarks and references to Appendices
Witts	15/7/18		Equipment of Division issued for the second time after the Miraville battle.	
	16/7/18		Move from Witts to Rocquetoire. Administered by 11th Corps.	
	19/7/18		Move from Rocquetoire to Aire	
	to 25/7/18		General Routine Work	
	26/7/18		Entrained at Jalonne Begonne for Frévin Capelle	
	29/7/18		Detrained at Frévin Capelle. Administered by 9th Corps, and arrived at Arcis le Fonsart.	
	30/18		Arcis le Fonsart. General Routine Work resumed.	

Army Form C. 2118.

No 39

WAR DIARY
or
INTELLIGENCE SUMMARY.
(Erase heading not required.)

Instructions regarding War Diaries and Intelligence Summaries are contained in F.S. Regs., Part II. and the Staff Manual respectively. Title pages will be prepared in manuscript.

Place	Date	Hour	Summary of Events and Information	Remarks and references to Appendices

A.A. & Q.M.G.
50th Division
May 1918

4A 19/8/5
24 6/18

Army Form C. 2118.

WAR DIARY
or
INTELLIGENCE SUMMARY.
(Erase heading not required.)

Erase ~~Volume~~

Place	Date	Hour	Summary of Events and Information	Remarks and references to Appendices
Beauvois	1/5/18		General Routine Work	
	to		"	
	26/5/18		"	
	27/5/18		Move from Beauvois to Revillon	
"	27/5/18		Revillon to Acheux le Poissonnet	
			Acheux le Poissonnet to Esthaon	
	28/5/18		Esthaon to Romigny	
	29/5/18		Romigny to Billes Augers	
	30/5/18		Billes Augers to Igny le Jard	
	31/5/18		Igny le Jard to Le Breuil	
			Le Breuil to Vert la Gravelle	

Instructions regarding War Diaries and Intelligence Summaries are contained in F. S. Regs., Part II. and the Staff Manual respectively. Title-pages will be prepared in manuscript.

WAR DIARY
or
INTELLIGENCE SUMMARY.
(Erase heading not required.)

Army Form C. 2118.

Parts 50 D Vol 37

Army Form C. 2118.

WAR DIARY
or
INTELLIGENCE SUMMARY.
(Erase heading not required.)

Volume

Instructions regarding War Diaries and Intelligence Summaries are contained in F. S. Regs., Part II. and the Staff Manual respectively. Title pages will be prepared in manuscript.

Place	Date	Hour	Summary of Events and Information	Remarks and references to Appendices
Netly Ford	1st to 9th		General Routine Work and refitting the Company & station	
Mondement	10th to 17th		General Routine Work	
Beauvais	18th to 30th		Refitting of Divisional Artillery and M.G. Battalion. On the 28th 16 18pdr Guns and 5 4'5" How" Received	

Army Form C. 2118.

WAR DIARY
or
INTELLIGENCE SUMMARY.
(Erase heading not required.)

VOL 38

Volume 40
MAJOR A.A. ROTH 50th DIVISION
DADOS July 1918
for

Place	Date	Hour	Summary of Events and Information	Remarks and references to Appendices

Instructions regarding War Diaries and Intelligence Summaries are contained in F. S. Regs., Part II. and the Staff Manual respectively. Title pages will be prepared in manuscript.

Army Form C. 2118.

WAR DIARY
or
INTELLIGENCE SUMMARY.
(Erase heading not required.)

Place	Date	Hour	Summary of Events and Information	Remarks and references to Appendices
Huppy	1/7/18		Refitting of Division still in progress	
	6/7/18		"	
	5/7/18		Move of 106 Field Coy R.E. and 75th Field Ambulance from 50th Division to 1st Army for administration	
	6/7/18		Administered by 22nd Corps	
			Move of 6th Yorkshire Regt. and 6th South Wales Borderers from 50th Division to 11th Army	
	12/7/18		Move from 50th Division to 22nd Corps Troops:-	
			H.Q.s. 150 I.Bde.	
			Nos 1, & 4 Coys 50 Div Train	
			3rd Field Ambulance	
			50th Divl Artillery Coys ble with:-	
			7th & 47th Field Coys R.E.	
			2 Sections 50 M.G. Bn.	
			X + Y 50 Inf Bdes Heavy	

WAR DIARY
or
INTELLIGENCE SUMMARY.
(Erase heading not required.)

Army Form C. 2118.

Place	Date	Hour	Summary of Events and Information	Remarks and references to Appendices
Suzanne	14/7/18		Move from 50th to 30th Division of 6th Cheshire Regt. and 6th South Wales Borderers for instructions from DDMS II Army	
Martin Eglise	15/7/18		Move from Suzanne to Martin Eglise. Administered by DDMS 40th Lof6 (South). Arrival of 73rd & 54 Stats Wales & 4th K.R.R. Corps from Sequence to Martin Eglise for administration as a unit of the Division	
"	17/7/18		Move from 50th Division to Sequeux Camp:— No 2. Coy A.Vet Corps, 2 Field Ambulance, 151 Mobile Vet Section for administration	

WAR DIARY
or
INTELLIGENCE SUMMARY.
(Erase heading not required.)

Army Form C. 2118.

Instructions regarding War Diaries and Intelligence Summaries are contained in F. S. Regs., Part II. and the Staff Manual respectively. Title pages will be prepared in manuscript.

Place	Date	Hour	Summary of Events and Information	Remarks and references to Appendices
Martin Eglise	17/8		Move from 22 Corps to Abancourt:- No.3 Coy Asbops. O/Secl 50 m/Boy	
"	19/8		Move from Abancourt to Martin Eglise: 6th Royal Engineers Trg as unit of Division. Move from 9th Corps Trps to 50 Division: 3rd Field Ambulance. No.4 Coy ASbops. 47 Field Coy R.E.	
	23/8		Arrival of No.2 Coy Divl Train & 50 Mob Vet Section from Lignereux	
	29/8		Cease to administer Abancourt Lignereux Camps	
	31/8		Move from 50 Division to 18th Division of 50 m/G.Btn. 50th Division complete with Infantry Btns and all units now administered. Transfers from other sources complete.	

WAR DIARY
or
INTELLIGENCE SUMMARY.

Army Form C. 2118.

Volume #1

WAR DIARY
A ROTH
A Sqn
A24 Guns 1918
Major T.B. Gully

Vol 39

Army Form C. 2118.

WAR DIARY
or
INTELLIGENCE SUMMARY.
(Erase heading not required.)

Instructions regarding War Diaries and Intelligence Summaries are contained in F. S. Regs., Part II. and the Staff Manual respectively. Title pages will be prepared in manuscript.

Place	Date	Hour	Summary of Events and Information	Remarks and references to Appendices
Martin Op Togisc	1/8/16		General Routine Work	
	6		for the Month of August	
	31/8/16		Administered by DDOS 2 of 6 (South)	

Army Form C. 2118.

WAR DIARY
or
INTELLIGENCE SUMMARY.
(Erase heading not required.)

Vol 40

Volume No 43

Major A. A. ROTH. A.O.D
D.A.D.O.S
50th Division

Army Form C. 2118.

WAR DIARY
or
INTELLIGENCE SUMMARY.
(Erase heading not required.)

Instructions regarding War Diaries and Intelligence Summaries are contained in F. S. Regs., Part II. and the Staff Manual respectively. Title pages will be prepared in manuscript.

Place	Date	Hour	Summary of Events and Information	Remarks and references to Appendices
Martin Eglise	1st		} Mine at Routine Work and H. Field Ambulance reported 50th Division	
	6th			
	15th			
Lucheux	16th		Move from Martin Eglise to Lucheux Administered by AOC 17th Corps and DOOS III Army	
	15th(a)		Move from 22 Corps to 50th Division of SAA Section 50th DAC	
	19th		Conference held with Staff Captains of 149 & 150 Bdes	
	21		" " " " 50th Bn MGC and everything found satisfactory 151 Bde	
			Inspection of Lewis Guns to complete to 30 per Bn. Issue of those for AA purposes including those for AA purposes	
Montigny	26th		Move from Lucheux to Montigny Administered by 13th Corps and IV Army	
Combles	28th		Move from Montigny to Combles	

Army Form C. 2118.

Army Form C. 2118.

WAR DIARY
or
INTELLIGENCE SUMMARY.
(Erase heading not required.)

Instructions regarding War Diaries and Intelligence Summaries are contained in F. S. Regs., Part II. and the Staff Manual respectively. Title pages will be prepared in manuscript.

Place	Date	Hour	Summary of Events and Information	Remarks and references to Appendices
Corbelio	29th		Administered by ADOS III Corps.	
	30th		50th Division complete with all tactical and essential equipment	

Army Form C. 2118.

WAR DIARY
or
INTELLIGENCE SUMMARY.

(Erase heading not required.)

Volume XX   Vol 41

DIARY
of MAJOR AA ROTH
50" Division
DADOS October

Army Form C. 2118.

WAR DIARY
or
INTELLIGENCE SUMMARY.
(Erase heading not required.)

Instructions regarding War Diaries and Intelligence Summaries are contained in F. S. Regs., Part II. and the Staff Manual respectively. Title pages will be prepared in manuscript.

Place	Date	Hour	Summary of Events and Information	Remarks and references to Appendices
Lucanson	1/9/18		Administered by ADOS 13 Corps.	
	2/9/18		7th Divl Artillery attached for Ordnance Services	
	3/9/18		12th Divl Artillery " "	
	5/9/18		Move from Lucanson to Epehy	
Epehy	6/9/18		7th Divl Artillery transferred to 7th Division	
			Six Lewis guns issued to 151 Brigade HQs to replace lost in action	
			Twenty three Revolvers issued 150 Bde "	
			One Vickers Gun issued to 50th MGBn to replace lost in action	
	8/9/18		Leather Jerkins received and issued to various units	
			Two Vickers Guns issued and replaced lost in action	
	11/9/18		Move from Epehy to Gouzeaucourt Farm	
	12/9/18		Move from Gouzeaucourt Farm to La Fin Aux Soldats	
Gouzeaucourt Farm	14/9/18		6th Divl Artillery transferred to 12 Division	
			Eleven Lewis guns issued to 1st KOYLI to replace lost in action	

WAR DIARY or INTELLIGENCE SUMMARY

Army Form C. 2118.

Place	Date	Hour	Summary of Events and Information	Remarks and references to Appendices
La Spur Braxhodale	14/10/18		Issues of Guns Lewis to r/m units in ratio as stated	
		8/18	1 to 13 Black Watch	
		11/18	10 to 4" K.R.R. Corps	
		11/18	3 to 13 Black Watch	
		13/98	5 to 2nd R. Dub. Fus.	
		14/10/18	6 to 6th Inns. Fus.	
	15/98		50 Dist. Artilly. transferred from 12th Division to 50th fd Ordnance Services	
	16/8/18		Conference with Staff Captain 151 Bde. by D.A.D.O.S.	
			Two Lewis Guns issued to 2nd Dub. Fus. (to replace lost in action)	
			Four " " " " 2nd Northd " " " " "	
	17/9/18 to 21/9/18		Progress made with issues of white clothing to all units of Division	
	22/8		Eight Lewis Guns issued to 2nd Dub. Fus. to replace lost in action	
	18/78		Six Lewis Guns issued to 3 Royal Fus. to replace lost in action	
	23/18		15 pdr Gun of B/250 Bde R.F.A. condemned by storm	
			18 pdr. Gun received for B/250 Bde R.F.A.	

WAR DIARY
or
INTELLIGENCE SUMMARY.
(Erase heading not required.)

Army Form C. 2118.

Place	Date	Hour	Summary of Events and Information	Remarks and references to Appendices
La Tron Vaux Soldats	24/8		Lewis Guns issued to 2 Mons Fus to replace lost	
			" " " " 6th Lanc Fus " "	
			" " " " 4 KRRC " "	
			" " " " 1 Roy Fus " "	
	25/8	16 pdr	Gun of 6/250 Bde condemned by Iorv & demand.	
			Further progress made with issue of winter clothing	
		18 pdr	Gun of C/250 Bde replaced	
	26/8	18 pdr	Gun and carriage condemned of C/250 Bde R.T.R.	
			Gun and carriage issued to C/250 Bde R.T.R. in replacement	
			Further progress made with issue of winter clothing	
	28/8		General Routine Work	
	29/8		" " "	
	31st		Move from La Tron Vaux Aux Soldats to Le Cateux	

SECRET WAR DIARY VOLUME 45 Army Form C. 2118.
or
INTELLIGENCE SUMMARY.

Vol 42

DIARY OF
MAJOR A.A. ROTH, ARMY ORDNANCE DEPT.
DABOS — 30th DIVISION
NOVEMBER 1918

D.A.B.O.S.
30th DIVISION

WAR DIARY
or
INTELLIGENCE SUMMARY

NOVEMBER

Army Form C. 2118.

Place	Date	Hour	Summary of Events and Information	Remarks and references to Appendices
Acheux	1/11/16		Administrary for 1. ANZAC XIII Corps	
	1/11/16 to 5/11/16		Gauge Routine work	
	3/11/16		Days with rainward staff sergeant put taken in charge proceed to the forward positions in sectors in Q.5.4, Q.3/69 and as 2/1/18 B Noir Rail frames & aired casualty of indirectary shown—	
			13 Lewis Guns to guns for carrying out refits	
			500 magazines	
			15 Smith 11½" Chothing & gases shortings	
			60 Rifles it Bayonets	
			40 Steel helmets gas	
			Same (more) the dump of 8 Lewis Guns part 3 Boots pinaforts	
	6/11/16		Office moved forward to Warloy Factory	
	7/11/16		Officer went forward to situated on the 1st round 1st army R.O. for Cachés with 74 Lewis Guns said new complete & Suns	

WAR DIARY
or
INTELLIGENCE SUMMARY.
(Erase heading not required.)

Army Form C. 2118.

Instructions regarding War Diaries and Intelligence Summaries are contained in F. S. Regs., Part II. and the Staff Manual respectively. Title pages will be prepared in manuscript.

Place	Date	Hour	Summary of Events and Information	Remarks and references to Appendices
Fontaine au Bois	8/11/18		In order to increase transport of supplies, carts and commandeered returned to Bavai —	
	9/11/18		Certain lines including Bavai-Quievrain turnpike etc. left unfilled by troops are reserved as demands. Orders issued not to put out of running to repairing parts	
Noyelles	10/11/18		Officers to port of stores moved forward to Noyelles & teams ordered to rejoin by 10th August.	
	10/11/18		Chk R — of stores moved at Noyelles — Also undergoing abolished on this date.	
			Same having passed to it place possible on (3⁰) (0ch) Black water	
			1st ½ R	
			4th × R R	
	11/11/18		Office moved forward to Bavai —	
	12/11/18		Stores moved forward to Bavai—	

WAR DIARY
or
INTELLIGENCE SUMMARY.
(Erase heading not required.)

Army Form C. 2118.

Place	Date	Hour	Summary of Events and Information	Remarks and references to Appendices
Amiens	17/10/18 to 2/11/18		General Routine work. Inspection of men at Diebouch Chateau for the clothing etc & Issue to Russians of same.	
	20/10/18			
	24/10/18 30/10/18		Started to equip Pete to 21 pr and received R.E. vans & Church's for same because I had nothing & very few lorries. Shortage of most kinds of kit & urgent need of clothing as lot of men & of men's stores & blankets of all kinds but specially warm clothing, but equip clothing of huts	

WAR DIARY
or
INTELLIGENCE SUMMARY.

(Erase heading not required.)

Army Form C. 2118.

DEPOT 60D

543

ROYAL ARMY ORDNANCE CORPS

MAJOR A. A. ROTH, R.A.O.C., O.B.E. (M)

DECEMBER 1918

VOLUME A6

WAR DIARY or INTELLIGENCE SUMMARY. VOLUME 46

DECEMBER — Army Form C. 2118.

Place	Date	Hour	Summary of Events and Information	Remarks and references to Appendices
Flanders	1st – 12th		General Routine work — Supply of stores from Base delayed on account of shortage of trucks	
"	12th		Units being in urgent need of stores, Capt. arranged for lorries to proceed to Rouen. I proceeded on this date to Rouen to superintend the matter	
"	13th – 19th		General Routine work — Certain stores received from Base & issued to Units	
Le Quesnoy	19th		Move of office & stores to Le Quesnoy	
"	19th		Arrival from Rouen of lorries with stores including Clothing Books etc	
"	19th – 31st		General Routine work — Stores received & issued in satisfaction of Units demands	
"	31st		Conference held G.S.O., A.A. & Q.M.G. etc regarding equipment of units supplies Alterations thereto	

Army Form C. 2118.

WAR DIARY
or
INTELLIGENCE SUMMARY.
(Erase heading not required.)

ROYAL ARMY ORDNANCE CORPS
JANUARY 1919

MAJOR A.A. ROTH. OBE. RAOC

D.A.D.O.S 50TH DIVISION.

VOLUME 47

Place	Date	Hour	Summary of Events and Information	Remarks and references to Appendices

Army Form C. 2118.

WAR DIARY
or
INTELLIGENCE SUMMARY.
(Erase heading not required.)

Place	Date	Hour	Summary of Events and Information	Remarks and references to Appendices
Le Quesnoy	1.1.19 to 31.1.19		Administered by AOOS XIII Corps. General Routine work	

Army Form C. 2118.

WAR DIARY
or
INTELLIGENCE SUMMARY.
(Erase heading not required.)

RAOOS 50 R

Vol 45

ROYAL ARMY ORDNANCE CORPS

MAJOR A. A. ROTH, O.B.E.

FEBRUARY 1919

VOLUME 48

Place	Date	Hour	Summary of Events and Information	Remarks and references to Appendices

WAR DIARY or INTELLIGENCE SUMMARY

Army Form C. 2118.

FEBRUARY 1919

Place	Date	Hour	Summary of Events and Information	Remarks and references to Appendices
Ouesnoy	1.2.19		Administered by ADOS XIII Corps	
	28.2.19		General Routine Work	
	20.2.19		Commencement of return of certain stores for demobilisation	
	25.2.19		Commencement of erection of huts for Intermediate Collecting Station	
	25.2.19 – 28.2.1919		General work in connection with demobilisation	

WAR DIARY
or
INTELLIGENCE SUMMARY.

Army Form C. 2118.

ROYAL ARMY ORDNANCE CORPS.

MAJOR A. A. ROTH

MARCH 1919.

VOLUME 49

WAR DIARY
or
INTELLIGENCE SUMMARY.
(Erase heading not required.)

Army Form C. 2118.

MARCH 1919

Place	Date	Hour	Summary of Events and Information	Remarks and references to Appendices
Ad Quarry	1/3/19	—	(On award HAA. XIII Corps) Intermediate Collecting Station formed adjoining Railway line at Ad Quarry Station	
	10/3/19		General Routine work	
	11/3/19 - 13/3/19		Instructions received to equip 3rd Regns R.E. to mobilization scale for service abroad. Stores prepared by Corps Inspection Committee in accordance with Army Demobilization instruction	
	14/3/19			
	15/3/19 - 23/3/19		General Routine work	
	24/3/19		Lorry loaded with Binoculars, Compass, watches (returned by Units) despatched to Calais in accordance with Corps Instruction	
	25/3/19 - 31/3/19		General Routine work	

11

RAODOS 50 D

Vol 47

Censored

WAR DIARY
or
INTELLIGENCE SUMMARY
(Erase heading not required.)

Army Form C. 2118.

ROYAL ARMY ORDNANCE CORPS

LIEUT. F.A.E. PINE

APRIL 1919

VOLUME 50

WAR DIARY
or
INTELLIGENCE SUMMARY.
(Erase heading not required.)

APRIL 1919 Army Form C. 2118.

Instructions regarding War Diaries and Intelligence Summaries are contained in F. S. Regs., Part II. and the Staff Manual respectively. Title pages will be prepared in manuscript.

Place	Date	Hour	Summary of Events and Information	Remarks and references to Appendices
Le Quesnoy	1/4/19 – 14/4/19	–	Administered by A.D.O.S, XIII Corps. General Routine work	
"	15/4/19 – 30/4/19	–	Administered by D.A.D.O.S, Avesnes Sub area	
"	17/4/19	–	Lieut. F.A.E. PINE, R.A.O.C, took over charge of I.O.S. on departure of Major A.A. ROTH for Avesnes Sub area	
"	29/4/19	–	All lorries returned to 50 Kyd. L. Coy. in accordance with 50 Kyd. Packet Q848 of 28/4/19	

W Pine Lieut
I.C.
OO D Guesnoy